LET YOUR LIGHT SHINE

Let Your Light Shine

by

Anthony Smith MRCVS

Illustrated by Philip T. Robinson

The Pentland Press Limited
Edinburgh · Cambridge · Durham · USA

© Anthony Smith MRCVS 2000

First published in 2000 by
The Pentland Press Ltd.
1 Hutton Close
South Church
Bishop Auckland
Durham

British Library Cataloguing in Publication Data.
A catalogue record for this book is available
from the British Library.

ISBN 1 85821 763 6

Typeset by George Wishart & Associates, Whitley Bay.
Printed and bound by Bookcraft (Bath) Ltd.

To Cameron Gibson MRCVS
Veterinary Surgeon, Author (Alexander Cameron)
and Minister in the Church of Scotland.

He has inspired and encouraged me.

Contents

Foreword

by Michael Clarkson, DVSC, PhD, BSc, DSHP, MRCVS

Formerly Professor of Farm Animal Medicine, Liverpool Veterinary School and President of Veterinary Christian Fellowship.

ANIMAL STORIES fascinate most of us and when their owners become involved as well, the interest is more than doubled because so often they are 'characters'. Throw a vet into the plot and you're sure to have a winner! This book has all these ingredients and more. The vet is a Yorkshireman who has worked in Lancashire for twenty years, the stories are from his wealth of experience of dealing with animals in the Pennines and the owners are the strong-minded characters who work the farms in this rugged region. Stories which deal with the harsh realities of farming, involving birth, sickness, healing and death, demonstrating the bonds that exist between animals and owners, which the vet is invited to enter. The farmer who is convinced that the vaccine you recommended and sold him hasn't worked because his calves are dying. The call to lamb a ewe miles away at a lonely hill farm when you're tired and hungry. The wish to encourage a vet student to deliver a calf by Caesarean operation in the middle of the night. Through these and other good stories, the bond between farmers, their animals and their vet is revealed and enjoyed.

What makes this book more than just good stories is the extra bond which is introduced, that between creation and Creator, humans, animals and God. Anthony Smith is not only a vet but a Christian and in a natural way, each chapter concludes with a brief postscript, encouraging readers to start and develop this relationship as well as enjoy the stories. I have greatly enjoyed both stories and postscripts and am sure that others will do so, too.

ACKNOWLEDGEMENTS

*To my wife, Wendy, for sacrificing togetherness while I was shut in
my writing room and for listening to the first renditions.*

*To my daughters – Lucy for her very exacting proof reading and
Mary for her sincere and encouraging comments along the way.*

CHAPTER ONE

Faith in Practice

AS WE MADE OUR WAY across the wet tarmac from the church to the little village hall, we were impervious to the darkness and drizzle of an autumn evening in the Pennines. The thrill of the singing, the preaching, the testimony and, above all, the vigour of that last hymn, still resounding in our minds, had been so uplifting that we were oblivious to such inclemencies. The combined congregations of four or five local churches had sung, 'Tell out my soul, the greatness of the Lord,' with such enthusiasm, aided and abetted by the organist masterfully coaxing the full measure of each succeeding harmony from his instrument, that we must nearly have lifted the roof off the old church! As always on these occasions, we could look forward to an ample supply of tea, cakes and biscuits in the hall, while in excited chatter, we relived the highpoints of the service, keen to savour them for days to come.

Our little group of churches was on the fringe of the diocesan area of the cathedral in Rutherford, an industrial city about twenty miles away. The cathedral staff had initiated a revival mission in the area, to encourage new commitment and forestall any danger of fossilisation of the congregations who gathered regularly, week . . . by week . . . by week.

George Carter was a well known itinerant evangelist who had been invited to take a prominent part in the month-long mission.

1

All eyes had followed him as he climbed up into the pulpit, floppy black Bible in hand, to deliver his galvanising sermon.

'In another few weeks, it will be Christmas,' he began, 'and during all the carol concerts, nativity plays and midnight masses, wherever we come from tonight, we're sure to find ourselves singing that great hymn, "O come all ye faithful". A shifting mutter of nodded agreements was the polite response from the packed pews.

'Well that's great,' he continued, 'great to have faithful people. Faith is a precious gift – you can move *mountains* with it!' he added, raising his eyebrows and pausing, for dramatic effect. 'If you're a believer in Jesus Christ,' he continued, 'then that hymn is for you, because you are counted – with the faithful. But,' he said, lowering his voice and clasping the edge of the pulpit with one hand, 'but – I'd like to remind you of some words in the epistle of St. James – "Faith without deeds is dead".' He intoned the words again, more slowly this time in case we needed a further reminder, 'Faith – without – deeds – *is dead*!' We all jumped as he shot out the last word, its impact accentuated in the silence that followed. The cathedral staff exchanged glances across the aisle, evidently pleased by the effect their man was having.

George Carter straightened up, adjusted his gold-rimmed glasses and smiled, as if to reassure the flock that he wasn't about to devour them. The church relaxed as he went on, 'Let's consider for a moment what we mean by "faith". I'm sure you'll all recognise that faith isn't about sitting on a fence wondering whether or not you're a believer, and wondering just how much of the Bible you should believe or not believe. No, faith only becomes a reality, a foundation in our lives, when we jump down onto the side that says, from now on, Jesus is my Lord and Saviour, and I want to build my life on his example.' He paused to allow a few throats to be cleared and then, leaning precariously over the top of the pulpit, he asked, 'Do you think a person can then live a Christian life, simply in his own human strength? Is faith all that is needed?' A few more coughs were offered in response and every eye was fixed on the motionless evangelist. 'Not a bit of it,' he said, regaining a more upright posture, 'he or she would fail at the first little difficulty they encountered! No, our faith needs to be supplemented by a generous helping of divine grace.'

'It is by grace you have been saved,' he cried, waving the big Bible aloft, 'grace through faith! Have you ever thought about God's grace?' he enquired, lowering his tone again. '"Amazing grace! How sweet the sound that saved a wretch like me."' He allowed the words of the well-known hymn to echo round the building, and then returned to its concept. 'Grace; graceful; gracious; social graces even.' He savoured each word to allow its beauty, richness and meaning to sink in. 'Our God is a very gracious God,' he crescendoed, and then, threatening to fall right out of the pulpit this time, he added passionately, 'Dear men and women, brothers and sisters, how we need that same grace to shine out of our lives if we're going to make any impact for Christ in this wicked world.'

The congregation tensed for a moment as these personal words scored a direct hit, but relaxed again as the preacher warmed to his theme and enthralled them with the life stories of Christian men and women who had made their faith work – sometimes within international organisations promoting health and education perhaps, sometimes unsung heroes in a small area or community.

Finally, sensing that the hearts of his hearers had been well and truly warmed, George Carter reiterated his punch line, the text with which he had begun, 'Faith without deeds – is dead,' delivering, for effect, the last word in an empty and hopeless tone. 'Just – dead. Now then,' he resumed, more brightly, 'we don't want any rigor mortis setting into the church, do we?' A few brave souls dredged their throats for a smile and a final cough or two.

'May I invite you,' he continued, 'to plead with Almighty God, to make it clear to you how you're going to spend the rest of your lives for him? I mean you as an individual' – his eyes surveyed the pews, penetrating even the recessed ones – 'and also, you as a whole church.' He retrieved his glasses from the very edge of the lectern and casually allowed his glance to fall on the cathedral staff. 'I'm not trying to say that you're not putting your faith into practice already,' he said, 'far from it, but from time to time it's a good thing reverently to ask the Lord if some new effort, some new direction or some new endeavour is needed. It won't be easy but just remember, God doesn't have any conscripts in his army – just volunteers . . . like you and me.' With that, he had quietly withdrawn to his seat, and the congregation was left to reflect a while before the last hymn was announced.

Later that night, I took my customary walk down the track, giving our two dogs their last outing before bedtime. The orange lights of the little town where I worked were twinkling down in the valley, but up on the hillside where we lived, it was very dark and still. Inside, however, my heart was still aglow with some indefinable flame, and while the dogs busied themselves with some new-found scents, the words of the evangelist kept repeating themselves in my head. He'd said something about putting faith into practice, and as I worked in veterinary practice, those words had found a lodging place in my mind. I wanted to lay hold of the moment before sleep supervened, morning broke and I launched into another day's work on the farms.

I leant on the glistening gate post and closed my eyes. 'Lord,' I began hesitantly, 'I really enjoyed that service tonight and it's done something inside me. I don't want to lose the strength of those words so please, Lord, show me how I can use my life and my work for your glory. Amen,' I added, with a slight lump in my throat.

Whistling the dogs, I headed back up the track feeling a new lightness in my stride and a contentment in my face. My prayer had been informal and short, but it had been sincere and heartfelt and I felt an assurance that God had accepted it. 'Ah well,' I thought, 'I've given it all to God – it's in his hands from now on.'

CHAPTER TWO

A Tough Business

AUTUMN IS THE TIME of year when we begin to contemplate the approaching season of winter through the rose-tinted memories of summertime. The cattle are still outside, cudding comfortably on the dew-soaked pasture. Early morning mists lie undisturbed and columns of smoke rise vertically from cottage chimneys. Those of us who work on farms are easily beguiled by the muted sunshine and warm hues of autumn leaves. It's far more agreeable to look back to summer shows and long evenings, to remember curlews, peewits and hay-making, than to look forward to the cold dark days ahead. We fall for it every year, however, and have to wait for the first gales before we are at all prepared for the stark reality – summer has gone and winter is almost upon us. Winter demands clumsy green waterproofs and electric lights, and only returns muddy farmyards and chapped hands.

The second week in November was the one that did it – three full days of an unrelenting gale of a wind which tore its way through the trees and roof-tops, shredding every last leaf from the thrashing branches, twisting off dead wood and blasting cascades of raindrops against the windows. It was hard work just to listen to it, but to work in it was exhausting and exasperating. Vets who work on farms become quite adroit at standing in the yard, leaning against the car and balancing on one foot in order to change into boots and over-trousers, but the wind is always thrusting to sweep your second wellie into the dirty puddle. After that, as you reach inside the car for your coat and stethoscope, you have to guard against a suddenly slamming door or boot lid. Having reached your patient and the security of a building your composure needs to be at its most controlled as latches rattle and straw scatters. Stripping off for a calving soon brings out some unmanly goose-pimples in the summer-softened skin!

Oxenbeck Hall was a natural target for such conditions. You couldn't say it nestled against the hillside – that would be far too comfortable a description for a farmstead with such a bleak backdrop as Houghling Moor. The nineteenth century industrialists had had no influence in this locality as they had done just a couple of miles down the valley, and apart from one narrow strip of tarmac and some drystone walls which were no longer repaired, the whole area must have changed little since the date when 'B.M.H. 1674' was chiselled into the lintel above the front door. Pasture land which had once been wrested from the wilderness finally gave way over the uppermost walls to the bent, sedge and reed of the moorland which swept away into the distance and the greyness of a Pennine skyscape.

The title 'Oxenbeck Hall' suggested far more grandeur and opulence than had ever lodged there, but it was nevertheless an arresting building because of its sheer solidity. Walls which were three feet six inches thick at ground floor level were joined by massive interlocking cornerstones, and narrow panes of glass were compressed between deep wedge shaped mullions. The slates never rattled or loosened because the roof was stone too, an enormous weight bearing down on the ancient, hidden timbers. It was certainly well built and well proportioned, but any pretence of grace or elegance was finally dismissed by the outer veneer of industrial black, blown up the valley from factory chimneys and etched into the millstone grit by the acid rain of decades.

Buttressed up against one gable end, and similarly heavily built, were the barn and shippons, low-roofed cow houses the width of the building, with stone-flagged floors and standings for about ten cows. This arrangement must have withstood the test of time, but in the early seventies, extra buildings had been needed to house the increased numbers of stock now being carried by the farm. In accordance with the climate of grant-aided farm expansion then in vogue, two large buildings made from steel spans, concrete blocks and corrugated asbestos sheets were erected. They stood across the now concreted yard, facing the old Hall and buildings which they could comfortably accommodate twice over. Built on slightly rising ground, they overpowered the old Hall by their height and span but after a mere quarter of a century, the asbestos of the new sheds was beginning to darken and fracture, and several holes were already apparent. The old stone building would easily outlast its modern, airy counterpart.

Oxenbeck Hall now had tenants who worked in Rutherford, and the farm had been amalgamated with its neighbour, so Brian Cormack, the new owner, only spent part of his time there, mainly looking after the cattle in the winter. He travelled between the farms and the outlying land dressed in very work-weary clothes and driving one of the most battered Land Rovers in the county. He was a large energetic man, one of the first in the area to abandon dairying in favour of beef cattle and hill sheep. For company he had his farm man Jack Hudson. Once a mill worker who had 'escaped' to the hills, Jack was only ever referred to as 'Hudson'. Brian often chewed a stem of straw during the long intervals between their infrequent dialogue, while Hudson mouthed a dirty, flattened, home-rolled cigarette in between his frequent attempts to ignite the thing.

'Right, Hudson, get four bales out fo' t'sheep – be sharp!' Brian might say, while he shouldered a heavy bag of barley to feed the store cattle. A full ten minutes would elapse before a new topic was broached.

'Watter trough's owerflowin' – 'ave ah to fix it?' Hudson offered generously.

'Nay – leave that – get some straw darn – there's sucklers to go round next,' would be a typical rejoinder.

I had done the tuberculin and brucellosis tests there a month ago – Monday and Thursday afternoons for the first group, and Tuesday and Friday afternoons for the second. Each group had about ninety suckler cows with calves at foot, and also the stock bulls. When I say 'calves at foot', I mean calves born in the spring and early summer so that by now they were strong, sizeable though unhandled animals, used only to the freedom of the vast acres of that wild hillside. The herd would have been gathered in the morning and then the three of us would attempt to split off the calves and pen the cows in the yard. The noise created by a herd of cows bellowing for their calves, augmented by the youngsters' reply, was almost deafening. Cow muck was scattering everywhere in panic, and the gates of the cattle crush crashed brazenly as Hudson fearlessly trapped each cow for me to inject and blood-sample. I shouted out the ear-tag numbers and hoped that Pauline, who was listing all the details, could hear above the hubbub.

When winter came, we were glad that that particular job had been put behind us. The labelling of blood samples and the recording of numbers in wet, windy and cold conditions is a nightmare as everything soon becomes covered in a dirty film of cow muck, grease and water.

By late November, however, the calves had finally been spayned, an agricultural term for weaning which is an especially

10

stressful time for the calves as they are separated from their mothers and housed – both of which are novel and scary experiences. This was the situation to which I was called one blustery, wet tea-time. Brian had made his customary check of the calves as he gave them their ration, only to find one animal dead and two others in severe respiratory distress. They were standing open-mouthed, with foaming saliva round their faces, gasping and wheezing for breath. The diagnosis was self evident – bovine viral pneumonia; it was well understood by both of us and didn't need to be articulated. Brian lived with the problem and probably knew as much about treating it as we did. This year, however, we had persuaded him to spend a lot of money on a comprehensive vaccination programme, and the calves had been injected twice before they came inside.

Brian eyed the corpse where they had dragged it out onto the bare concrete yard. 'Nah what dost tha' think o' thi' bloody vaccine – eh?' The question was cruel because it was delivered to be taken personally – a sort of revenge after apparently wasting hundreds of pounds and having only a carcass to show for it.

I thought that I'd better do a post-mortem, not to verify the cause of death, but to collect some samples of lung tissue for the lab to work on. Avoiding his glance, I communicated this decision to my client and started for the Land Rover to get my PM knife.

'What abah't these two?' he shouted after me, clearly upset that I wasn't about to dispense an instant remedy for the two badly affected calves. 'I'm thinking,' I shouted back through the wind, nearly as curtly.

My post-mortem examination revealed a pair of lungs which looked and felt more like boiled beetroot than the light raspberry mousse which they should have resembled. The airways were full of froth produced by the infection in the lungs, and so the poor creature had effectively drowned in its own sputum.

'Is there anywhere I can wash my hands?' I asked afterwards, holding my dirty knife out in front of me. 'Ay – there's a tap just inside shippon door,' was the dismissive reply. 'It's nobbut cold mind.'

I crossed the yard and pushed open the old wooden door and fumbled for the tap in the gloom. I let a couple of yards of brown, rusty water splash onto the floor before rinsing my hands and knife, and then dried them as best I could on a pile of old paper sacks.

'Ah've just bi'n studying,' said Brian, leaning over the gate, 'an' there's one or two more startin' bi t'luke on it, see.' *He'd* noticed what *I* was expecting, and what I'd planned to look for next. I was wrong-footed by the way he was retaining control over the course of the visit. It's nearly always the case that if one calf of a group is obviously affected, there will be several others in which the disease process is not yet so well developed, and which therefore need treating as soon as possible.

'I'll be back with some injections,' I said, pulling my sleeves down again and veering off into the wind. I collected a pocketful of injectables from the Land Rover and returned, vaulting the gate to get one jump ahead. 'Come on then, Brian,' I said, 'let's get these two bad ones done first.'

Hudson had been casually standing by all this time, gaining a quiet satisfaction from my discomfiture and from the few puffs of smoke he had managed to raise. Like an alert dog, he reacted automatically and abruptly to his master's voice, 'Get thi'sen ower 'gate – vet'll need an 'and.'

The bunch of eighteen calves showed a mixture of fear and excitement as the three of us entered the territory of their winter quarters, and proceeded to cavort round the place, kicking their

heels and 'barking' – it was too high spirited to be called 'mooing'! As the bedding was tossed, so the dust rose and sure enough, a cacophony of coughing assaulted our ears. It was an unwholesome sound to a stockman, and the distress of the two badly affected calves was a stark witness to the power of respiratory infection.

We tried hard to catch them in a corner, but the poor animals allowed their adrenalin to override common sense and made a dash for freedom, only to worsen their already desperate shortage of breath. It wasn't very pleasant to overcome them through exhaustion, but at the second attempt, we were able to collar them, inject them and release them to stagger back to their fellows. By this time, we had made a mental note of four others that had that subtle stress in the way their ribs moved, and we set about catching them too. Their flow of adrenalin was well established now, and our only chance was to outwit them, these four-wheel drive, all-terrain bundles of power.

Brian and I drove one of the four round the outer wall, hoping that Hudson would be able to catch its head as it braked for the corner. The calf got halfway towards him, smelt a rat, turned tail and bolted before he could make a move.

'Tha'll 'ave to be quicker than that, Hudson,' was Brian's glancing remark as we circled the pen for a second attempt. One of the basic laws of medicine is 'at least do no harm', and as the calf was clearly becoming stressed, I wondered if we were actually worsening the situation instead of relieving it. Brian, however, had no such reservations and, spreading his arms and legs widely, attempted to threaten and usher the calf towards our chosen corner. The calf obliged for a moment, then slammed into reverse, turned and made his escape. 'Nay, bloody hell, Hudson, tha's let it slip ageean – get that fag art o' thi' mouth.'

Hudson impassively transferred the disgusting weed to his shirt pocket as we let the mob of calves settle down, allowing the sporadic coughing to subside.

'Fetch a gate,' was the next curt instruction, 'bi sharp,' and Hudson climbed out of the pen and vanished into the darkness of the yard. He soon reappeared struggling against the weight of a twelve foot gate and the thrust of the wind. We heaved it over the fence and tied one end into a corner so that it made a hinged, makeshift catching pen. Hudson was stationed at the free end, ready to close it in on my patient as soon as Brian and I drove it in from behind. I selected one of the poorly group and with everybody concentrating on the same one, we cajoled it round the outer wall once again, away from the other seventeen. It saw the trap too late as, with split second timing, Brian and I shoved hard up behind and Hudson nipped in with the gate.

The confused animal got its head stuck through the bars of the gate, bellowed and took a standing leap, but we would be able to hold it for a few moments. There was absolutely no possibility or point in examining it, this resentful, impetuous adolescent. Act first – think later, or not at all, is the motto of suckler calves. Brian couldn't help himself saying, 'Come on, vet, get it jabbed!' but I was well aware of the need for speed, and already had the syringes loaded. I managed to put the two injections into the tensing muscles, put a coloured marker down its back and then Hudson released his pressure on the gate and the calf turned and ran. We repeated this operation on the other affected animals and withdrew for a breather.

'Now what'll 'appen?' asked Brian, rubbing his two days' worth of stubble. Predictions about the outcome of pneumonia outbreaks are notoriously unreliable, even nowadays with the more specific treatments we can choose from.

'I don't know,' I answered, 'but we can't do any more for them now. I'll be back tomorrow afternoon to see how they're getting on. Will two-thirty be all right?'

'It's Carlthwaite market tomorrow – tha'd better mek it four o'clock.' That'll be nice, I thought to myself, it'll just have gone dark again by then, but aloud I said, 'Let me know in the morning if there's any deterioration.'

Next day dawned more brightly, and the gale was reduced to an ordinary wind which propelled thick rags of clouds across a blue-patched sky. The roads were full of puddles and debris and spotlit circles of light chased along the hillside where the sun penetrated the tears in the cloud. By late afternoon, however, the darkness was gathering fast and it was with a sense of foreboding that I trundled up the track to Oxenbeck Hall.

I was not disappointed in my apprehension as it was easy to see where another body had been dragged across the yard, the carcass laid up against the old barn, ready for the knackerman to collect. Mr Cormack appeared round the corner of the building looking like he was about to blow a fuse.

'So much for thi' bloody injections then,' he said, coming out of the shippon door. A hollow laugh emphasised the point, backed up by a sideways expectoration. I couldn't blame him in a way; most of his next year's income was represented by these calves and besides the money, a lot of effort and expertise went into bringing the farming wheel round full circle, year after year, with hardly any let-up for illness or holiday.

I looked suitably contrite and got into my waterproof working coat, directing my attention into the group of calves. Clearly, one of the worst cases from last night had died, but the other showed some improvement. As I continued to look, I could make out that the calves we had treated and marked also looked better but another couple were starting to show signs. There was no alternative but to repeat the operation, giving five calves their second dose, and the two new cases their first.

I needed to be personally responsible for an outbreak like this, so, after injecting each calf, I made an appointment to visit again the following day. Then, perhaps, I would be able to leave Brian and Hudson to finish the series of injections by themselves.

'Tha'll not be chargin' for all these visits,' said Brian bluntly.

'Well, somebody will have to pay for them,' I replied as pleasantly as I could.

'What abar't cost of all that vaccine then?' he shot back.

'You'll have to take my word for it that *without* those vaccines, you'd probably be in a lot worse trouble than you *are*,' I replied, and with that, I strode off back to the Land Rover. 'See you tomorrow,' I called over my shoulder.

Thankfully, the remaining calves did eventually make a good recovery, though they certainly lost their bloom and took some weeks before they looked full of bounce again. At this stage, Brian owed the practice a lot of money and after several reminders, the account balance was still rising, and I was left with no option but to call at his farmhouse and see if I could draw a cheque. Like all small businesses, we were very dependant on everyone paying their way.

I got out of the Land Rover just as Brian was tying his two sheepdogs to their kennels in the yard. 'What dost tha' want this time,' he said, rather more harshly than was necessary, I thought. As he straightened up, I ventured that I was merely wondering if he could let me have some money, his account being rather overdue.

'Cum into 'ouse,' he said gruffly, and I followed him into the kitchen where he took off his dirty coat and sat down at the table. 'Whear's cheque book at?' he asked his wife, who duly left the stone sink, dried her hands, and got the pile of bills from the drawer in the dresser.

He extracted the cheque book, tossed it across to me and located the practice invoice which turned up with an obvious, red reminder sticker on it. He studied it carefully for a moment before declaring: 'Ah don't know 'ow yer' dare charge prices you charge,' and with a mortified expression on his face went on, 'yu' must think farmers are made o' money.'

'Well,' I explained, 'modern drugs are better than old-fashioned ones, but of course they do cost a lot more money, and anyhow,' I added, 'you must admit they did work pretty well.'

'Knock twenty quid off then,' he said, passing me a pen. I bartered for ten pounds and then, honour done and duly signed, conversation lightened and we had an amiable discussion about the weather, the family and the price of spare lambs.

As soon as it felt not too indecently hasty to make my departure, and with dinner time rapidly approaching, I got up and made my way across to the door.

'While thar't 'ere on a free visit,' said Brian, reaching for his coat again, 'just cum down t'yard, and 'ave a luke at mi 'ouse cow. It wouldn't tek its feed this mornin' . . .

On Reflection

Life can be a tough business all right. For some, like Brian Cormack and Jack Hudson, and for thousands like them, life is physically tough. For others, in leadership or management for instance, it's mentally tough, and for others, looking after sick children or elderly relatives perhaps, it's emotionally tough. For some, there is a combination of all three but for all of us, at some time in our lives at least, we need an element of resilience if we are to win through.

When we go to a service in church or chapel, whether it is to a wedding or funeral, or to ordinary Sunday worship, we are usually met by a sense of dignity, order, calm and peace, and when the door shuts behind us, it's as though the hustle and bustle of the workaday life has been left outside. Is this what the 'opiate of the people' is all about? Is this some form of escapism, a giant con trick with which we sustain ourselves from week to week? What possible relevance can church, hymns, sermons and Bible readings have for a person whose normal environment is tough, demanding, dirty, relentless and lonely?

The answer is that they have exactly the same relevance to people like that as for all of us. The world in which we are privileged to live is often beautiful, colourful, exciting and fulfilling. It also contains some awful horrors – pain, suffering, squalor, poverty, violence, indecency and abuse to name but a few.

We are told that in heaven, '[God] will wipe away every tear from their eyes. There will be no more death or mourning or crying or pain, for the old order of things has passed away.' (Rev. 21:4) Does that imply that until then, we're stuck with the 'wicked world' which George Carter alluded to in the opening pages, and we'll just have to put up with it? Surely not! What hope Jesus puts in our hearts when he teaches us to pray:

'Thy kingdom come, Thy will be done
On earth as it is in heaven (!)'

In these familiar words, we can catch a glimpse of the enormous gulf which exists between good and evil and between heaven and earth, and we become aware of our responsibility to 'live and work to his praise and glory'.

One of the great messages of the gospel, a word which means 'good news' by the way, is the bringing back of mankind into fellowship with God. St. Paul calls it reconciliation through Jesus Christ. '. . . God was reconciling the world to himself in Christ, not counting men's sins against them . . . We are therefore Christ's ambassadors, as though God was making his appeal through us.' (2 Cor. 5:19 & 20)

Anyone who makes light of the Christian faith by disparagingly referring to people being 'religious' or 'do-gooders' or the 'Jesus wants me for a sunbeam brigade', or some such phrase, has absolutely no notion at all of what is at stake.

To be ambassadors for Christ in this sometimes dark world, we need God's strength to be at work within us. The New Testament is full of words like perseverance, endurance, steadfastness, faithfulness, commitment, determination, and words with a similar tone. We can only acquire these qualities from God himself, in the ways he has ordained for us such as studying the Bible, prayer, praise and by coming together in Christian fellowship. Jesus often withdrew into lonely places to be with his father in prayer, but he also told us not to babble, thinking we should be heard because of our many words. (Matt. 6:7) This should encourage us to make a start with short prayers, on the bus, in the middle of a walk, at coffee break – in fact at any time (when we're not supposed to be concentrating on something else of course!).

I don't believe that God wants a bunch of softies in his church, an army of flower arrangers, coffee club Christians and bring-and-buy-sale organisers. (I'm speaking very tongue in cheek!) On the contrary, we need a tough faith to live in a tough world, but that toughness can only come through yielding our hearts to him, as clay in the potter's hands. He needs to shape our attitudes and motives and to reinforce us with love and compassion before we can be strong in the faith, members of a strong church that continues to make an impression on our fellow countrymen and

A TOUGH BUSINESS

women, and to make an impact on our national life. Wherever there is darkness, God calls someone to stand in the midst of it, to shine into it the light of his glorious kingdom. It could be you or me. Let's make sure we're spiritually tough enough to do the job. Let's not be afraid to 'let our light shine'!

CHAPTER THREE

Keeping in Touch

A S A NEW GRADUATE in my first practice, I remember it being impressed upon me to 'Keep ringing Nellie!' 'Don't forget to phone back to the surgery!' 'We'll get along fine so long as you remember to ring in!'

The practice was a mainly agricultural one and covered a wide area of countryside. I soon knew the whereabouts of every phone box in the district and I carried a tin of old pennies for the purpose of 'ringing Nellie', the receptionist, secretary, medicines dispenser and general factotum. 'Any more visits Broadley way?' I might ask. If the answer was 'No', I knew I could safely return without having to face an irate senior partner, or, even worse, pass him on the road, storming along to an urgent case very near to where I had just been!

One of the greatest boons of the last few years is the electronic pager, or bleeper, as it is colloquially called. This little black box sits in your pocket and listens – waiting for its unique phone number to be dialled. Without having to wonder how far I've got on my round and which farm to ring, Pauline, the receptionist at the Colston practice, can bleep me at the press of a telephone button. Whether I'm driving along, attending to an animal or having a chat and a 'brew' in the farm kitchen, the bleeper springs into life, alerting me to the need to contact the surgery. In years gone by, Pauline used to have to anticipate which farm I would be at and then try to ring me there. Sometimes I had already left, and sometimes the farmer's wife would be blocking the line with a long conversation. Some farms have an outside bell, but by the time the farmer had dashed out of the buildings and across the yard, it was often too late.

No, the bleeper has been a great innovation, and when it's sitting quietly in your pocket, it's a great comfort and reassurance to know that all is well back at the practice, and that there's no need to entertain that niggling worry at the back of the mind that some farmer might be jumping up and down, waiting for a vet to come and calve his cow.

Lambing time in our practice used to be a nice compact but intensive season running from about the middle of March to the middle of April. Nowadays, however, we have some pedigree flocks that lamb early, in order to have well-developed ram lambs ready for the September sales. This adjustment to the breeding season has been made possible by hormone treatment of the ewes back in July of the previous year, allowing them to be 'tupped' a good six weeks earlier than nature would naturally allow.

Early one evening, around the turn of the year, with Christmas cards still adorning the office, and tins of biscuits from well-wishers still lying around anywhere they could find space, we started to think about setting off for home after a busy day.

We had had a few days of that bitter cold weather which makes it impossible to keep warm unless you're doing hard manual labour. Thermal underwear might be efficient, but when combined with thick socks, hairy shirts and a body warmer, coming into the office soon makes you feel dirty and cumbersome. Darkness, freezing winds and wet are our worst enemies when working on farms, and I was saying to Roger that although it was my night 'on duty', I wouldn't mind going home and having a hot shower, followed by a good meal and a 'feet up by the fireside type' of evening.

'Don't be such a wimp,' he said with a twinkle in his eye. 'We're here to give a good service and anyhow, we need the money!' He could afford to be smug – his night on duty wasn't until Thursday, three days away!

I locked the cellar door behind him and turned to meet Pauline standing with a worried look on her face and a notebook in her hand. 'Sorry,' she began, 'but Julie Barker has just rung in – they've got a lambing. They've no transport – could you go out there straight away?'

'Right,' I said sweetly as she went to enter it in the day-book, 'mark it for me will you?' But to myself I said, 'I wonder if I've got time to go home for tea first – the Barkers always panic a bit early with their Suffolks.'

Roger was right of course, we're in practice to give a good service, but now and again a little self-pity has to be dealt with first.

'I'm hungry.'

'I hate their farm – the yard is always muddy and windy and we only ever seem to go there in the dark.'

'I was in their village an hour and a half ago, why didn't they phone then?'

I resolutely put these thoughts out of my mind and went back out into the cold to make some final checks in the back of the Land Rover. When you're on duty, you need to be fully stocked with all the things you might need in the night – there's nothing worse than having to open up the surgery in the small hours when if you'd been properly prepared, you could have been well on the way to the farm. Pauline reappeared at the top of the steps. 'I've just had Julie on the phone again, wanting to make sure you were on your way.'

My emerging expletive was eclipsed as she continued, 'I said you were just leaving.'

'I just am,' I replied, retreating back into the warmth to put on my boots and over-trousers. Anxious clients like the Barkers are best humoured by a dashing arrival at the farm, the vet already booted up and stethoscope in hand!

As I drove away from the surgery, and broke the wrapper off one of my emergency biscuits, I started to concentrate on the job ahead and even felt ever so slightly proud that the whole large animal department was now dependent on me for the next fourteen hours, but I was well equipped and had reliable support from my reception team. Pauline would be off home now, leaving Sheila in charge of the phones and evening surgery. Later, the practice phone line would be diverted to Gordon and Joan, a retired couple who answered the phone at home, right through till morning. Answer machines might be all right for some businesses, but in our type of work, a client with a sick animal needs the assurance of a human voice.

After a few more miles, I crested the brow of the hill and the lights of the village came in sight across the valley. I pictured the Barkers fretting and agonising as the empty minutes ticked by. Raymond Barker was an ex army man but even retired and in his seventies, he could still do a decent day's work on his smallholding, perched on one of the contours of Lowther Hill. His wife was rather a diminutive figure, occasionally seen through the kitchen window bent over some culinary task, but their daughter Julie was the one who had most interest in the sheep. So exclusive and so perennial was her interest, that her poor Mum and Dad had almost given up hope of ever becoming grandparents! I remembered that their yard was small so I knew to reverse down the steep track, carefully avoiding the big stone gateposts and parking strategically out of range of the hosts of Midian which, in the form of very hairy border collies, prowled around their dark kennels and strained at their chains.

Raymond greeted me cheerfully, seemingly immune to the cold in his leather gloves, green woollen hat and thick greatcoat tied up with the regulation belt of baler band. I sorted out some bits of equipment, purposely leaving the big interior light on as I shut the back door. If I needed to come back for anything, it would be a difficult lambing indeed, and that light would somehow be a reassurance in the shadowy darkness of the farmyard.

We entered the old shippon and shut the door against the freezing wind which whipped round the yard. The standings between the boskings had been bedded up and gated off to convert them into lambing pens. The clean straw reflected a soft warm light, intensified by the low ceiling, and there were a few contented bleatings from the ewes which had already lambed. Any suggestion of a nativity scene never made it to my consciousness, however, as the ewe in the first pen was obviously in trouble, a worried look on her face accompanying a distressed panting. Tell-tale bits of string hung under her tail.

'Eee,' said Julie with an enormous smile, 'I'm right glad it's you – we all'us have good luck when you come!' I hope I'm not about to shatter that confidence I thought to myself, conscious of how often pride comes before a fall. My disquiet grew as she went on, 'We've got two strings on lamb's legs but it won't even get started.' I hate lambings where someone else has done much more than put a hand in: by the time the vet arrives, there's usually some swelling in the passage and all the slippery amniotic fluid has leaked away, making the vet's job much harder.

I pulled on a long plastic sleeve as Raymond and Julie laid the ewe on her side and with a handful of lubricant gel, I gently began to feel my way inside. I soon got Julie's strings unhitched and out of the way, thereby gaining a fraction more space in which to work. The lamb's front legs were nicely in the passage but the head simply wasn't following. Exploring deeper into the ewe, I eventually located the head which seemed to resist being drawn towards me. With more lubrication, I managed to pass my soft plastic noose over the back of its head and apply some traction.

Conscious of Julie's sublime faith in my abilities, I pulled with one hand and guided with the other but no – this head was resolutely not going to slip into the pelvis. Is this the time to change tactics and embark on a Caesarian, I wondered, mentally baulking at the thought of taking ages over an operation which is so much quicker and easier back at the surgery where we have all the luxuries of good light and hot running water? I persuaded myself that it was more a question of misalignment than plain oversize which was preventing the birth of the lamb, so I tried again, this time repelling and flexing one leg back into the womb before pulling on the head noose again. This time the head promptly plopped up into the pelvis but Raymond and Julie, blissfully unaware of what was going on in their sheep, were fortunately spared the next anxiety – how was I going to retrieve that leg? The head and one leg nearly filled the pelvis now, but working my fingers gently alongside them I could just touch the flexed knee. A little more and I could almost hook it with a finger. No room. Pressure beginning to deaden my hand. The ewe was not helping now as in her discomfort, she made agitated attempts to jump up. After two more attempts, I succeeded and was able to withdraw my hand, stretching the leg into its proper place alongside the other. The relief was palpable and with a little extra pull, the lamb slithered out onto the straw, shook its head and took its first gurgled gasp of air.

'What's that noise?' said Julie, but attuned as they were, my ears had not missed the ascending tones emanating from the bleeper, deep in my pocket.

'Sounds like somebody else wants me,' I explained, 'that's the surgery bleeping me.'

'Thank goodness you got here first,' she said breathlessly, adding, 'that's right grand getting a live lamb like that!'

I gathered up my tackle and quickly dried my hands before making for the door.

'Thank you ever so much!' said Julie effusively.

'My pleasure,' I replied, adding innocently, 'can I leave you to give her some penicillin – just in case?' Just in case Julie's technique hadn't been quite as clean as it should have been, I thought.

'Certainly you can,' she answered, smiling hugely, 'thank you – thank you!'

They were much more interested in their new arrival than in seeing me off so, with the yard tap frozen and nowhere to wash my boots, I climbed into the welcome light of the Land Rover and rang Sheila on the car phone.

'Sorry to disturb you,' she said, her voice coming over loud and clear, 'but I've got Les Morton here. He wants to pick up something for a calf with navel ill.'

Good, I thought with relief, it isn't another visit, and gave her some instructions as to what to dispense. Modern communications had saved Sheila from having to entertain an impatient farmer during a busy evening surgery and had reassured me that there were no more urgent calls. With that comforting knowledge, I set off up the track, turned onto the little road through the village, and started to look forward to my evening meal which I knew would be waiting for me. Wives are a wonderful asset to people with a job like mine, I thought, always ready with a warm kitchen and a meal that could be accelerated onto the table, served on time, or put back into the oven and delayed until I got home.

Before long, however, the phone on the dashboard rang and jerked me back into reality. Rightly guessing that I would now be on the road, Sheila had rung the phone directly this time, bypassing the bleeper.

'Sorry,' she said with concern, 'I'm afraid I've got a pony with a bit of colic at Mayfare Stables – could you give Mrs Shilton a ring?'

I pulled up on the verge and took down the number.

'Thanks, Sheila,' I said, 'I'll phone you back and let you know what I'm doing.'

I dialled Mrs Shilton and got the engaged tone. Fancy asking you to ring them back and then blocking the line! How tiresome, I thought. I tried again in a minute or two – still engaged! This was ridiculous, and I could feel myself becoming just a tiny bit edgy. Another call might come at any moment and here I was wasting valuable time. I decided to drive on to the next junction where I would have to decide – eastwards for home or southwards for Mayfare stables. I drove on, stopped and tried again. Ah! – a ringing tone! Good! It rang...and...rang... and I thought, 'Oh no! The lady must have gone back to see her pony – how exasperating!' I let it ring on, hoping against hope that there would be an outside bell in the yard.

Suddenly there was a crumping sound, followed by a mixture of fumbling and heavy breathing, and eventually a small boy's voice managed, 'He – hello.'

'Hello,' I said calmly, hiding my emotions with great skill, 'could I speak to Mrs Shilton please – it's the vet.'

I didn't know whether he had caught that last bit because without a word of acknowledgment, I heard the phone being put down, and in the background, a door shutting. I hoped with all my heart that he was running down the yard to get his mother.

Business phones often have taped music which trips in if you have to be put 'on hold'. This outfit was no exception and I was now treated to the unmistakable strains of 'Coronation Street', and I imagined the television glowing from amongst the clutter of well worn furniture, horsey magazines and tack which characterise the living room of many equine establishments.

The door banged again and soon, to my intense relief, it was Mrs Shilton saying, 'Is that the vet?'

'Yes,' I replied, 'I tried to ring you earlier – but you were engaged,' I added pointedly.

'Oh, yes,' she said, 'I was just ringing mi' friend – she's good with horses.'

That's rich, I thought – who needs a vet with friends like that! 'Well anyhow,' I continued patiently, 'tell me about your pony – when did it first show signs of colic?'

'He's been a bit restless since late on this afternoon, but he's just done some droppings – will he be all right now?'

'It depends,' I said, thinking aloud, 'does he look any easier?'

'Well,' she said, 'he's got quite a sweat on, but he's not rolling any more.'

Colics can vary from quite mild tummy aches to devastatingly painful blockages of the bowel which can lead to death in a matter of hours. The passage of droppings was good news, but not necessarily the end of the episode. To visit the animal now might be a little hasty but I knew from experience that to go home and try to eat my meal with a serious case on my mind was only likely to give *me* a bout of indigestion! I reached my decision and said, 'I'd better come and check him over – better safe than sorry. See you shortly.'

I quickly used the phone again to tell Sheila of my decision. 'Could you phone Wendy and tell her to put my tea on hold,' I added.

'Right-oh,' she said, 'and I'm just putting the phones through to Gordon and Joan, so I'll tell them where you're going.'

'OK,' I said, 'see you tomorrow.'

'I hope you have a quiet night after this,' she said. 'Bye.'

Twenty minutes later the Land Rover bumped into the frozen yard and as I switched off the engine, all fell silent. With a deliberate effort, I got out into the cold night air and reached for a clean overall. I hoped they wouldn't notice my boots, still with some bits of Barkers' bedding stuck in the treads.

I went across to the only lit stable and peered over the door. The floor revealed the unmistakable evidence that the occupant had colic – churned up dirty bedding caused as the animal had pawed the ground and circled the box in an attempt to find relief. The pony himself was steaming gently from his sweat-soaked neck and his thick stable rug was stained and twisted from his attempts to lie down and roll. His head was low and he looked as though he'd just finished an endurance test over mountain and moor.

'Looks like you've been having a hard time,' I said, pushing my way in through the stable door

'We've walked him up and down the yard to stop him rolling,' the owner explained. 'He wasn't getting no better so we rang you, but he hasn't tried to get down for about half an hour now.'

'OK, old chap,' I said quietly, lifting the pony's head. 'Let's give you a check over.'

He jerked his head back and widened his eyes for a moment but he was in no mood to misbehave and he soon relaxed to my presence. I slid my stethoscope under his rug to listen to his heart rate – one of the best indicators of the severity of a colic.

'That's nice and relaxed,' I said reassuringly and moved along to his flank to listen to his abdomen. I lifted his rug and leant my ear to his side, immediately tuning in to the soft music of bubbles and tinkles which emanate from a normal horse's insides, orchestrated by the slowly rippling contractions along the intestines.

As I completed my examination with a few more checks, I began to feel confident that the worst was indeed over. 'I think things are getting back to normal,' I said, and observed the relief on Mrs Shilton's face, 'but I'll give him an injection just to be sure.' I went out to load a syringe with some spasmolytic injection.

'Just hold his head like that, will you,' I said, 'so that I can put this into the bloodstream.' The pony hardly flinched as I penetrated the jugular vein, and in a few moments, the injection was completed.

'Right,' I said brightly, 'he'll relax nicely when that gets working in ten minutes or so. Will you take his hay and water away and keep checking him till bedtime. If you're worried again, give me another ring. Otherwise, give him a nice hot bran mash last thing.'

'I hope we don't need to call you again,' was the reply, 'but thanks for coming out so quick.'

'It's all down to bleepers and mobile phones, Mrs Shilton,' I observed with some satisfaction. I got back into my shoes and was soon driving back along the road, the frosted verges glistening in the headlights. I pressed the memory button on the mobile to ring Wendy.

'Have you finished?' she said.

'Yes,' I replied, 'and I should be home in about twenty minutes.'

'I'll have tea on the table for you – but Lucy and I have had ours, I'm afraid.'

'I should hope so, dear,' I replied, 'but I hope you've left plenty – I'm starving!'

Modern communications make life so much easier, I thought, as I slipped the Land Rover into top gear and headed for home.

On Reflection

Keeping in touch with the surgery in farm practice is obviously very important – if the vet and the receptionist don't communicate, there will soon be some disgruntled clients and the vet will spend more time on the road than on the farms.

For the Christian, 'keeping in touch' with God is also very important, but how on earth can we expect to hear from the God of Heaven? We don't, for instance, expect to find messages from God left on voice-mail or on a fax! However, those of us who have sung the Prayer Book service of Matins down the years will be familiar with the words of Psalm 95: 'Today if ye will hear his voice, harden not your hearts.' The implication is clear, that it is indeed possible to hear his voice, but how can this happen?

Perhaps the first thing we need is an attitude of expectancy. If we aren't prepared to listen, then it's unlikely that we're going to hear very much! The mobile phone has to be switched 'on' before it can receive anything. The well known story of the boy Samuel in the temple illustrates how, when God called his name in the night, he thought at first that it was Eli, the priest. Knocking on Eli's door, he said, 'Here I am, you called me.' After the third time that this had happened, Eli realised that it was God calling the boy, and told him to answer: 'Speak, Lord, for your servant is listening.' Now there was a big difference: *your servant is listening* – and when that had happened, God could begin to communicate. (1 Sam 3:1-10)

Then we have to learn that God doesn't shout to make himself heard. We have to learn to listen within the quiet of our hearts, as perhaps Elijah experienced on Mount Horeb (1 Kings 19:11-13). After the tumult of the hurricane, then the earthquake, and then the fire, came the 'gentle whisper'.

Most people know the parable of the wise man who built his

house on a good solid foundation, and the foolish man who built his house on sand. (Matt. 7:24-27) Jesus compares the wise builder with 'everyone who hears these words of mine and puts them into practice.' Clearly, we have to hear his words before we can even begin to put them into practice.

The Bible is obviously a good place to start if we want to discern God's word for us – preferably with the guidance of a booklet of daily readings. With a little thought, and the illumination of the Holy Spirit, these verses gain a new dimension which lifts them off the printed page so that they acquire a gentle voice of their own, becoming for us spirit and life.

CHAPTER FOUR

While You're Here

'WHILE YOU'RE HERE – VET...', is a phrase which often crops up as a cue for a veterinary anecdote. No doubt this preliminary is current in the stories swapped within other trades and professions, but it has acquired a notoriety all of its own among farm animal practitioners. You arrange what you expect to be a sensible round of visits, try to oblige people by telling them what sort of time to expect you, and lo and behold, just as you're taking your overalls off, the farmer makes towards a doorway and says, 'While you're here...!' You can shorten a conversation about the weather or the political scene, but you try rebuffing a request to look at another animal! What makes it worse is that experience teaches you that what you look at as an afterthought is often far more serious than the case you originally came to see.

Jim and Joanna Sanderson ran one of our last truly mixed farms, Stoney Clough, a small farm overlooking Colston from one of the surrounding hillsides. With the exception of pigs, most species of farm animal were to be found at Stoney Clough, and Joanna was a regular caller at the surgery on their behalf. The sheep were represented by a selection of native breeds from Suffolks to Jacobs, and the beef herd included old dairy cows, a few lovely red Herefords and some modern, continental types. The variety of colours exhibited by the spring-born calves indicated the rich pool of genes which had contributed to their makeup. All these animals grazed happily together, sometimes using the fences as convenient rubbing posts. Not the perimeter fences, but makeshift jumps for the children's ponies. Their two girls, you see, were very involved in show-jumping and used these fences for practice. Not to be left out, Joanna also had a brood mare that had bred her several nice foals.

One Saturday morning, she rang to ask if she could collect something for one of the goats which had a sore teat. After discussing this in a bit more detail, I remembered that the sheepdog was due for its booster vaccination and a worm dose – would she like to bring Nell in when she came for the ointment?

'If that's the case,' she answered, 'I think you might as well come up here. Nell's a bad traveller and there's a calf could do with looking at – it's got a bad eye.'

'Right, I'll be up there in about an hour,' I said, thinking that that was just the sort of undemanding visit I liked on a Saturday morning. Saturdays often start with a more relaxed atmosphere than is usual during the week. The town is hardly awake and the waiting room hasn't yet filled up with people and pets. Both Roger and Pauline were off for the weekend, however, and so I knew that the peace could be illusory. Malcolm and I would have to deal with all the phone calls which the farmers made as they came in for breakfast. By the time we had charged down to the dispensary in the cellar a few times, however, morning surgery was well under way, with all the world and his wife wanting to see the vet or collect some medicine or other. We felt mightily relieved when we could leave the hubbub to our small animal colleagues and retreat into the peace of the countryside.

The Sandersons were great make-do-and-mend people, using all sorts of materials for repairs to their buildings and machinery. The show jumps were made from anything from old plastic barrels to broken telegraph poles, and a collection of dead Land

37

LET YOUR LIGHT SHINE

Rovers provided spare parts for their still roadworthy successor. While most farms had a cattle grid or a track running between walled fields, the approach to Stoney Clough was guarded by a pair of massive wrought iron gates, purchased for a song at a scrap metal dealer, and swung on a pair of home-made concrete gateposts of outsize proportions. As I opened them and drove through, I could see that the field looked empty so, knowing I would be back again in a few minutes, I drove slowly on. I bumped up the track of reclaimed tarmac and parked in the yard, uniquely paved with old flagstones, courtesy of Colston District Council.

The girls, Helen and Jane, were busily mucking out the stables, just about managing to give me a 'hello' between forkfuls. Their mother soon appeared, her work-weary clothes contrasting with her ruddy complexion.

'Mornin', Anthony,' she greeted me, 'what do you want to do first?'

'I'd better do Nell's vaccine to start with,' I replied, 'while my hands are clean.'

'Just watch yourself with her,' said Joanna, striding over to the old oil drum that, laid on its side, had been made into Nell's rusty lair. I loaded the vaccine into the syringe while Joanna gathered up the long dog chain and held her collar.

'Good dog,' I soothed, deftly sliding in the needle as Nell went rigid with malevolent indignation. She may not have been a good traveller by car, but when Joanna released her, Nell would have gone into orbit had her chain snapped!

I gave Joanna the worming tablet, explaining that it was best given after a small meal. 'You and Jim can do that later,' I said. 'Now, where's the next patient?'

'Oh,' she muttered, studying the little packet, 'oh, er, I have it fast in t'barn porch – over here.'

38

Crossing the yard, we found the goat tethered on some matted straw amongst a scattering of upturned buckets and a few hens. I bent down to examine her teat. 'This isn't so much a sore as a slow-healing cut,' I explained.

'Well, whatever it is, it makes her jolly awkward to milk,' said Joanna incisively. 'Can you stitch it up?'

'Not an infected cut like that,' I said, 'but it'll heal quite quickly under a bandage. Can you get me some warm water, please?'

In no time at all, I had the teat cleansed and wrapped in microporous tape. 'That'll be much more comfortable,' I said, admiring my dressing, 'and you'll still be able to milk her if you're careful.' Packing my things back into the box, I began thinking about my last case, the calf's eye.

'Let's have a look at the calf then,' I said as I shut the lid. 'Have you treated it yourselves at all?'

'We've put some of that there ointment in it,' she answered, showing me into the barn. The calf was in a wooden pen and had a permanent wink and wet cheek, typical of an inflamed eye. I climbed in and was in the middle of my examination when a door banged and Jim put in an appearance, smiling good-naturedly, his hands buried deeply in his overall pockets. After a diversionary preamble about the life history of the calf, his innocent smile broadened as he remarked benignly, 'Bull's a bit lame – I think you'd better have a look at it, while you're 'ere, like.'

'All right,' I said nonchalantly, and continued my instructions on how to treat the calf's eye. I climbed out of the pen and, facing Jim for the first time, realised that he wasn't joking.

Much as I hate pain and suffering, the idea of tackling a lame bull on a Saturday morning tested the mettle of my vocation to the limit. If only I hadn't mentioned Nell's booster, Joanna would have collected some teat ointment and I would never have known about the wretched bull! I wouldn't have minded so much if they'd asked me to look at the bull and, while I was on the farm, to please look at the goat, but surely it was unreasonable to lure me there with such a devious plan. Of course, it wasn't done on purpose, but it left me feeling rather a Noddy.

We went round to the cattle shed, and I entertained the thought that perhaps it was only a sprain, and that rest and confinement would be the treatment. The bull had a couple of cows for company, and their presence put the bull's stature in perspective. Everything about him was massive, especially his skull, neck and shoulders. Eighteen hundredweight of pure Blonde d'Aquitaine beef on the hoof, except that he was holding a forefoot, just resting the toe on the ground. Most unlikely to be a sprain, I thought, wishing I could just drive away.

Suddenly, I realised the significance of there being only two cows with him. I could picture the rest of the cows heading, as I spoke, for the freedom beyond those iron gates. 'I left the gate open when I came up,' I blurted out in guilty embarrassment, 'I thought I'd only be here for a few minutes.'

Jim evidently felt not the least twinge of conscience at this remark, but simply shouted for one of the girls. 'Vet's forgot to shut t'gate,' he said, 'just nip down on yer' bike and fasten it, Helen – he might be a while here.'

'They'll be OK,' said Jim, 'they were down bi' t'wood last time I looked.'

Relieved of that anxiety, my mind went blank as I tried to weigh up how to approach this afterthought of a case. Jim had his hands in his pockets, obviously convinced that the responsibility was all mine now. His chewing gum mildly irritated me.

'You won't have a crush big enough for him?' I ventured.

'Not really,' he replied. 'I'm doing a bit of welding on ours anyway – it were rusting through under t'floor.'

We usually 'drop' a bull using deep sedation, but that requires him first to be starved for forty-eight hours to reduce the bulk of digesting food in the abdomen. That seemed to be making a mountain out of what might be just a simple thing like a stone stuck in the cleft between the hooves. With no definite plan in mind, I told Jim to get a strong halter while I went back to the Land Rover for some tackle of my own.

'He's quiet enough,' said Jim when we met up again.

'Good,' I said – it was my turn to smile now – 'just pop that halter on him, will you?'

Jim squeezed between the bars of the barrier and approached the bull, studiously trying to arrange the halter as he sidled up to it. He made an initial attempt to apply it, but the bull dismissed it with an annoyed jerk of his head. Joanna reappeared at that point and, summing up the situation at a glance, entered the arena in a no nonsense manner.

'Whoa boy,' she said calmly, addressing the colossus while scratching his bottom with a stick. Jim retrieved his halter from under the bull's nose and tried again, completely missing this time as the bull ducked away to the side.

Regaining some confidence, and seeing the futility of the Sanderson team's approach, I decided to chance my arm and strode in with a noosed rope slung over my shoulder. No limply hanging piece of rope this, though, for this was my 'bull-rope', numb and heavy and it could have secured a battleship. I dropped it easily over his head and hurried to the nearest stanchion to get a purchase. The noose tightened commandingly as the bull jerked his whole weight back on it. Perhaps the pain in his foot warned him that his best course was to submit, albeit grudgingly, and so Jim and I were able to winch him in, one bight of the rope at a time.

'Right, Jim,' I urged, 'get that halter on now – we don't want to throttle him!'

Having secured him on the halter, we could ease some tension out of the noose and I began to feel a little more in control. The next problem was going to be how to lift that foot up in order to examine it. Jim was on the other side of the fence, still engaged in a knotty problem with his halter. Joanna stayed at a respectful distance. 'Do you need any water?' she offered.

'No, but a bale of straw to kneel him on would be a help,' I answered.

'I'll fetch you one,' she replied, and I turned my attention to the offending foot once again.

The impression grew in my mind that if I tried to lift that foot, the bull would wheel round and either squash me against the metalwork or give me a good pounding with his back foot – or both! Unravelling a second bull-rope, I managed to pass it round his waist and fasten it to another stanchion. The duped animal was now alongside the fence, securely anchored fore and aft. Joanna lugged the bale across, the bull was made to kneel his foreleg on it, and I set about his foot with my hoof knife. Aware of the hulk that I was now rubbing shoulders with, I was acutely conscious that he could call the shots any time he wanted, with a barrage of explosive resentment. With complete faith in the security of my ropes, however, I pressed on, carving off layers of hoof till I found that tell-tale black split, beyond which I knew would be a gathering of pus.

'Just get my torch out of that box, Joanna,' I said. 'You can shine it down here for me.'

My attention focussed exclusively on the circle of light as it illuminated the bull's foot and in particular, on that dark mark within it. Working rapidly, I soon had it opened up and was rewarded by a flow of pus.

'That should make him feel better in just a couple of days,' I said with relief in my voice. 'Just fetch me a bandage and that roll of cotton wool, please, Joanna.' We soon had the foot wrapped in a protective dressing and we released the ropes, allowing the battleship to sheer off to the feed rail, already beginning to bear a bit more weight on that foot. I gathered up my gear, feeling a surge of elation and fulfilment. That was a job well done, whether they realised it or not.

Evidently they didn't, because without any expressions of satisfaction or thanks, and without any offer of a cup of tea, Joanna helped me ferry my tackle back to the Land Rover while Jim disappeared back into the barn. I re-stowed all my various bits of equipment and peeled off my overalls with relief. I climbed up into the driving seat and Joanna closed the door on me.

'Don't forget to shut t'gate this time,' she said with a wink.

'Of course I won't,' I protested, adding with a grin, 'don't forget Nell's worming tablets, will you? Good luck!

On Reflection

'While you're here' jobs tend to be a nuisance in that your mind is geared to do certain tasks and it suddenly has to change wavelength and do something completely different. As well as worrying about getting delayed, you often feel that you haven't done your best because you're unprepared. It's surprising how much preparation we do in our minds through unconsciously thinking about the job ahead.

God, on the other hand, expects us to do quite a lot 'while we're here'. I mean 'while we're here on this earth'. Many of us will be familiar with the words of the creed which speak of Jesus being crucified, risen and ascended, after which 'he will come again in glory to judge the living and the dead'.

Before he comes again, however, we are urged to use our time wisely and profitably. Jesus himself tells us to use our resources productively in the parable of the talents. (Matt. 25:14-30) A talent was a quantity of money, but in the English language, it also conveniently encompasses the idea of gift or ability. Thus the man given five talents used it to double his money and was commended for being a 'good and faithful servant'. The man who had only been given one talent, on the other hand, dug a hole in the ground and hid the money. Jesus observed that the least he could have done was to have put it in an investment account and gained some interest. As it was, he had merely been caretaker to a 'hidden talent', for which Jesus called him a 'wicked and lazy servant'. I wonder how many hidden talents there are in the Christian church, gifts and abilities which God has given us and which lie undiscovered or unused.

St. Paul asks that God would 'encourage your hearts and strengthen you in every good deed and word'. (2 Thess 2:17) If we let those sentiments direct our prayers and the way we live, then there should be plenty of jobs to do 'while we're here'. If we keep our ears and eyes open as we go through each day, many opportunities present themselves when an understanding smile, a kind word or a good deed can bring a real blessing to another person. Well then, be encouraged! Let your light shine! It's not a chore. It's a privilege and a joy.

CHAPTER FIVE

A Bad Day

IT WAS FRIDAY AFTERNOON and it had been a hard day at the end of a tiring week. Some weeks are like that, when everything you do is only achieved with strain and difficulty. This particular Friday was keeping its grip on that pattern of events: one of those days when, as the locals say, 'Ah'd 'ave bin better off stoppin' i' bed!'

Roger was on holiday and Pauline was sending Malcolm and me criss-crossing around the practice as the phone hardly stopped ringing. A cow down here, a calving there, with a very poorly calf somewhere in between. We sorted out problems over the air waves so that Pauline could dispense various medicines back at base. All that on top of a round of previously organised visits, so that by four o'clock, after only a sandwich for lunch, I was feeling a bit ragged round the edges. Inspired clinical decisions had been displaced by that weariness and dullness of thought which makes you rely on experience and that built in automatic pilot which we all seem to possess. Not that my clients suspected that, of course; to them, I tried to seem my usual cheerful, efficient self.

The last booked call of the day should have been simple enough, merely the signing of a certificate, a straightforward enough task which didn't require too much computing power. The nature of that certificate, however, should have activated my early warning system. This was to be an export certificate and experience taught that export certificates have a nasty habit of causing problems. The Beckside herd of Friesian cows, in the ownership of E. Capstick and Son, was sending four pedigree heifers to a dairy farm in Spain. The blood tests had been done, official clearance arranged, and all that remained was a final health check within six hours of departure. The cattle lorry was due at about six o'clock, so I had arranged to go about an hour beforehand. That would avoid any complications should the lorry have been seriously delayed during the afternoon. Prematurely expiring certificates were better prevented than dealt with at midnight!

The beautiful June weather we had experienced recently had outlived its glory. As so often happens in the Pennines, the blue skies and heat had become dull, sultry and oppressive, and people hoped it would rain and clear the air. Even in the green hills, where it is usually fresh and earthy, the air now had the quality of a heavy vapour, and the beauty of the landscape had become flattened under a lowering sky.

I drew up into the yard and was greeted by Raymond Capstick who was gradually taking over the reins from his father, Ernest. 'Is it banna' rain or 'ow, does't 'a think?' he enquired, scratching his head through his cap.

'I think we'd all feel a lot better for a good downpour, don't you?' I said.

'Ah'll be sick if it does – ah've got eight acre down that ah want to git baled tonight. It can do what it likes once we've got that inside,' he replied resolutely.

'Well, I'll not hold you up long, Raymond – just a brief health check and then the forms to sign.'

'We 'ave 'em all ready for you,' he said, leading me off to a new building. Four immaculate looking heifers lay contentedly in a deep bed of clean straw. Raymond hooked his thumbs in his

braces and leant back on them in the manner of a man taking stock of his workmanship. It seemed a shame to disturb them but I needed to confirm the numbers on their ear-tags before signing any health certificates. 'Could we just run them behind a gate so I can check their ear numbers against the list?'

''Ow do you mean "check their ear numbers"? Roger checked them only last week when 'e took the blood samples!'

I didn't want to make a big issue out of the need to glance at a few numbers so I introduced a little diplomatic humour by saying, 'Yes, Raymond, *I* know that and *you* know that, but the Minister of Agriculture needs to know that they were checked today!'

The heifers carried on cudding without a hint of amusement, and Raymond's wan smile was cut short by the arrival on the scene of Ernest Capstick. I hoped my diplomacy had fared better than my attempted humour.

'Mr Smith says we've got to corner 'em up to read their ear tags ag'ean. Just hold 'is papers while I give him an 'and.'

You didn't have to be good at body language to tell that I wasn't endearing myself to the Capsticks that particular Friday. Ernest was walking with a wooden cane now, I noticed, and he hooked it on the fence with exaggerated resignation. Ah, well, I thought, it'll soon be all over and forgotten, and I jumped into the pen. I managed to creep up on one animal and read its tag while it was down – YW301-1070. I crossed back to the fence where Ernest was standing, and ticked off the number on the list. The other three heifers became suspicious, got up and stretched. Never mind, they'd easily walk behind a gate; they were very quiet. Two did, YW301-1036 and -1084. The third repeatedly baulked at the gate and shied away.

'Yer don't need to check that 'un any road,' said father. 'It's 1051, ah' know it is!' To doubt his word would have been to show lack of trust, but not to check the tag would have been professional negligence. 'There's no point in upsetting them,' he continued, 'it's too hot for that,' and he tried his best smile to bring me into submission.

'I'm sorry,' I said, 'but I need to check them before I can sign the forms. I'll just get a rope to loop behind her.'

'Well, I'll go to heck,' said Ernest, a hint of purple appearing on his frown as he banged my clipboard on the bars, 'we didn't have this trouble last year.'

As I hurried over for the rope, I reflected on the implication that last year, my colleagues Malcolm or Roger hadn't done their job properly. It's amazing how short memories can be, I thought. With a rope looped round her haunches, 1051 was soon persuaded into the narrow gap between the gate and the side of the pen, and of course, the number tallied exactly.

'Told you you were wasting your time,' said Ernest irritably.

'You'd best come into 'ouse to do the paperwork,' added Raymond, taking the clipboard from his father.

The old kitchen felt cool, with its low ceiling and flag floor. An old lady was sitting by the empty hearth in a studded brown leather armchair. She was reading the paper in a light to test the sharpest eyes. I wasn't introduced. 'Lemonade?' said Raymond, pouring some into a large mug.

'Thank you,' I said, disliking lemonade but anxious to be conciliatory. I spread my papers on the bare wood table, and my heart missed a beat as he thumped the mug down heavily beside me. 'That'll cool you off a bit,' he said, 'do you need a pen?'

I couldn't answer. My eye had fastened on the lab report on last week's blood samples. Oh yes, they were clear tests all right, as I had seen back at the practice, but what I hadn't spotted was that somewhere along the line, the ear numbers had become YV301s instead of YW301s.

'Now what?' asked Raymond, sensing that I was going to be awkward again.

I pushed the report towards him and pointed out the discrepancy, under which I was supposed to add my verifying signature. 'That's all right,' he continued, just slightly louder than was necessary, 'you can soon change the V into a W!'

The term 'vetting', has acquired connotations of thoroughness and unimpeachable integrity. To falsify a declaration would bring the profession as a whole into disrepute and the guilty individual would be struck off the register.

The old lady shook out a troublesome crease in the paper and under cover of the disturbance, I bleakly said that I couldn't make any alterations. Footsteps and a tapping stick presaged the arrival of Ernest as my mind shut down in self-defence at the latest hurdle. 'I've just seen t'wagon turning in off t'road,' Ernest announced, 'he's i' good time!'

Raymond explained the difficulty as I stared yet again at that list of numbers. 'You'll 'ave to sign,' said old Mr Capstick stridently, 'we'll be loadening 'em in a minute or two. Then they've got to be in Liverpool by midnight.'

'Sorry,' I said, slowly and deliberately to control the emotion and exhaustion in my voice, 'I can't sign the certificate with wrong numbers on it.'

'I'll tell thee what it is, Mr Smith,' began Ernest, tapping my chair with his stick. Oh, no, I thought. That phrase was always reserved for the extreme necessity of an ultimatum and my sweat glands reacted in anticipation. 'I'll tell thee what it is,' he repeated for added gravity, 'tha'll not be coming in this yard again if tha' doesn't sign. The Carlthwaite practice will be doing all our work in't future.' The tapping mercifully ceased. The old lady transfixed me with a glare round the edge of the newspaper.

'Look,' I began in forced restraint, 'can I use your phone? The

51

lab will probably be closed now but it's my only chance of finding out where the mistake is.'

'It's in't passage,' offered Ernest, waving his stick in the direction of a darkly varnished door. I grabbed the report and found the old-fashioned phone in a cubby hole in the wall. I dialled and waited, half hearing some muffled conversation in the kitchen as I stared at the dirty mark on the wallpaper where many a grimy shoulder had been rested over the years.

A voice eventually answered and relief flooded my face as I recognised the sound of Alan Threadgill, the director. 'I just came back in to collect some things I'd left behind,' he said, 'you were lucky to catch me.' I breathlessly explained to Alan the wretched impasse in which I now found myself, and he kindly went away to unearth all the original paperwork. He instantly spotted the typographical error and came back onto the phone. 'If you can fax me a confirmation of the correct ear numbers,' he said, 'I'll fax you back a new report form accordingly.'

'I think you might have saved my bacon,' I whispered. 'I'll dash down to the surgery – are you OK for twenty minutes?'

I returned to the kitchen and gathered up the papers, explaining my new plan as I did so. E. Capstick and Son looked at me with disgust as I gulped down the last of the lemonade. The lorry driver was standing in the doorway now, cutting off my retreat till I explained my predicament. 'I'll be back as soon as I can,' I said encouragingly, slowly squeezing my way past him.

The old lady put the paper down and offered to make him a nice refreshing pot of tea. 'I expect yu' could do without a hold-up on a Friday nee't,' she said to the driver, 'it must be very irritating for you. Milk an' sugar?'

I drove down the farm track and away to the surgery, my body tense, my face almost in pain. I exchanged the necessary faxes, checked and signed all the forms and then negotiated the Friday evening traffic as I made my way back to the farm as quickly as possible.

I know how time drags when you're waiting for somebody, and I wasn't surprised to find that by the time I returned, the heifers had been loaded and the ramp secured back in place. I tried a smile as I handed Raymond the clipboard for his signature. It wasn't reciprocated.

'Thanks fo' the tea,' said the lorry driver as he climbed up into the cab, the papers now safely clipped on the dashboard.

'You're very welcome,' Raymond returned, casting me a derisory glance.

It was now seven o'clock. I had delayed the lorry driver by nearly an hour and caused a great deal of despair. I had worked hard to try to redeem the situation but the fact remained, I was a nit-picking bureaucrat, not a farmers' vet. Large spots of rain began to fall as the sky grew yet gloomier. I put the sidelights on and manoeuvred quietly out of the yard.

When I arrived home, I felt stiff with tension and numb with exhaustion. I was too tired to eat and too hungry to go for a sleep.

'Isn't it foul out,' said Wendy as she opened the back door for me. I shook off my waterproof coat in the light of the kitchen. 'Have you had a reasonable day?' she enquired innocently.

On Reflection

Some Christians are very 'hail fellow well met' types of people. 'Allelujah, brother!' they greet you in the street. 'Praise the Lord indeed!' Maybe they have a broader and deeper faith than mine. Perhaps, on the other hand, they feel some insecurity. Whatever the truth is, our lives should indeed reflect some Christian spark of life, some real overflow of joy.

St. Paul says, 'Rejoice in the Lord always. I will say it again: Rejoice!' (Phil: 4:4)

The Old Testament says, 'Do not grieve, for the joy of the Lord is your strength' (Neh. 8:10), and in the Book of Common Prayer, we find in one of the psalms for morning service the words:

O come let us sing unto the Lord:
Let us *heartily rejoice* in the strength of our salvation. (Ps 95:1)

Simply dwelling on and voicing these words, has the effect of lifting our spirits and bringing a sparkle to our eyes (Praise the Lord!).

All this rejoicing, however, doesn't preclude us from hard days. Christianity isn't the great escape. Life is full of setbacks, difficulties, pressures and discouragements.

In the Yorkshire dales, the river Wharfe passes through a narrow rocky passage called the Strid. The water is compressed into the cleft and tumultuously churned into foam by underwater crevices and swirl pools. After a hundred yards or so of this, the rocky grip is released and the frenzied cascade suddenly finds its forces spent as it becomes a peaceful reach of pastoral river again. The piece of music by Smetana called *Má Vlast* (My Country), contains a depiction of the river Vltava. The orchestral representation of turmoil as the river passes over the rapids, and then the release, breadth and majesty which ensues further downstream, is a good mirror of the way our emotions can at times be both battered and delighted. 'Through all the changing scenes of life, in trouble and in joy...' is the way one hymn puts it.

What we need to remember is that when we are overfaced or under pressure, our minds are totally engrossed in the immediate. God, however, never gets too busy or so preoccupied that we become too insignificant for him.

Fear not, for I have redeemed you;
I have summoned you by name; you are mine.
When you pass through the waters, I will be with you;
and when you pass through the rivers, they will not sweep over you.

(Is. 43:1-2)

There's no need for Christians to feel any sense of failure when they go through a bad patch or a difficult day. We can battle on, with a certainty in the back of our mind that God is still with us, no matter how tired we feel. If, at the end of the day, we can pause to thank God for his presence and to count our blessings, we shall indeed find that 'the joy of the Lord is our strength'.

CHAPTER SIX

In Confidence

THE JANGLING NOISE woke me with a jolt, confused as to whether it was the alarm clock or the phone. I fumbled around in the dark and decided it was the phone.

'It's Mr Clarkson, High Laithe. We 'ave an 'eifer 'ere what can't calve. There's nothing showing yet – will it need a bit more time, d'you think?' I noticed it was ten to midnight.

'I'd better come and have a look,' I said, and repeated the name and address to make sure my drowsy brain had got it right. I sat up in bed and gazed into the darkness for a minute before heaving myself out into the cold. The brain picked up speed again and I remembered to phone our final year student, Heather, at her digs in the town.

'Calving,' I said, 'I'll call for you in ten minutes.' Some distant mutterings formed the reply, and I put the receiver down, briefly enjoying the satisfaction of sharing a rude awakening. 'She'll have to get used to it,' I mused, to justify my vindictive thought.

The process of waking up again was completed when we arrived at the farm, jumping out of the warm Land Rover into the cold night air which funnelled in from the moor.

The Clarkson brothers were lifelong bachelors whose rather dour demeanour suited their austere surroundings. Their ageing mother still kept house for them and the philosophy was that if things didn't change, they'd stay the same, which is largely what they did. Albert, the elder of the two, led us across the yard to an old stone building and climbed up a two-foot step of old bedding muck into a loose box. A beautiful red heifer stood among some clean straw, the glow of a cobweb-screened forty watt light bulb giving a warm ambience to the yellowing stone. The thick dust on the once whitewashed walls kindly reduced any small risk of glare to our night adjusted vision. Brother Hugh followed us with a bucket of water and some soap, and lifted these onto the ledge of a boarded-up window. Turning to the heifer, he grasped the halter rope and secured her to an old hay rack while I was discarding my pullover in favour of a waterproof calving gown.

'Just hold her tail, will you, Albert,' I said, using the soap to lather my arm, which I then proceeded to slide inside 'the passage', as it's modestly called.

'Ah've 'ad mi' 'and in,' offered Albert, 'an' ah could feel two feet, but no 'ead! That's when I decided ah'd better ring one of you chaps.' His smile expressed relief that the problem had been passed to me, and he leant into the heifer, expectorating neatly as if to seal the end of his part in the action.

'The reason you couldn't find its head is because it's coming backwards,' I answered, up to my elbow inside his heifer, 'I've got the calf's tail in my hand.'

'Arse f'ust! – aye, ah wondered that,' Albert interjected.

'And there's absolutely no chance of it coming through here,' I continued, 'it's far too big. It'll have to be a caesarian.'

'' 'Na then!' returned Albert, 'side door job, eh?'

Farmers didn't like posh names for veterinary terminology, and if a colloquialism could be found, it generally took over. Thus, a left displacement of the abomasum became a 'twisted stomach', while a cow with severe mastitis would be 'feloned', and a male animal, cut off in its prime, would be 'gelded'. So, 'side door' was the synonym of caesarian section, more common since the introduction of large continental beef bulls which bred correspondingly big calves.

'Do you mind if Heather has a feel?' I asked. 'She'll be qualified this time next year so she needs all the experience she can get.'

''Course she can,' said Albert, 'no good just watching.'

Heather soaped her slender arm and I tried to provide a commentary as she explored inside the heifer, giving nothing away to me as she gazed steadily up into the roof. I tried to get her to experience the gross discrepancy between the bulk of the calf and the narrowness of the mother's pelvis, but it's a judgement which comes with experience and I couldn't be sure if she was convinced. I didn't intend to try to calve it just to demonstrate the fact, however, as it was already well past midnight.

'Right,' I said, drying my arms on the hand towel, 'I want another clean bucket of warm water, and can we get an extension cable into here?' Hugh nodded and ducked out of the low doorway.

'Heather, get the op. box and the table out of the Land Rover, and then can I have the clippers and floodlight please. Come on, Albert,' I continued, 'give me a hand to push her against the wall – that'll give us more room and more light.'

'You don't put them out, then?' he said, putting his shoulder against the beast's haunches and heaving her sideways.

'No, far too dangerous to do that with cows and sheep – they'd choke and die. We just use local anaesthetic. It's much easier to do them standing up anyway.'

A caesarian isn't a terribly quick job even in daylight, and with all the preparation needed it could become a bit long-winded, so I had tried to convey a sense of urgency in my instructions. The extra equipment was soon lumbered through the door and up onto the deep straw, and the heifer pulled restlessly against the halter, unused to being restrained, and apprehensive about all this activity. The floodlight was hung from an ancient beam, only just above our heads, but it gave a comforting light and warmth.

'OK, Heather,' I said, 'it's all yours. What's your first job?' It was Heather's turn to look apprehensive now as she urgently tried to recall her lecture notes and to remember the one caesarian she'd seen a year ago with Roger.

'Clip up the flank,' she said after a moment's hesitation, and was shocked as a pair of clippers suddenly appeared in her hand. Hugh had rigged up the extension cable and in anticipation of the next problem, he let go of the halter and grabbed the loose plug out of the straw.

'There's nobbut one socket I'm afraid,' he explained, and swiftly exchanged the floodlight plug for the one from the clippers, plunging us all back into the relative gloom. Heather soon had the hair peeling off the left flank of the heifer, revealing a large area of clean, lightly coloured skin.

'Next job?' I asked, anxious to keep up the momentum.

'Local,' answered Heather, and was surprised to find a loaded syringe thrust into her hand.

'Here's one I prepared earlier,' I said with a grin, and grasped the bottle ready for a refill. 'Can we have the light back on, Hugh?' I asked.

When you're a student, there's a big difference between watching someone else do a procedure and actually being in control yourself. I could see her hesitancy, but she bravely overrode it by grasping the needle and striding back to the cow, which was once again bathed in light. With undue haste, she made to stab it in.

'Whoa!' I cried, my responsibility for her suddenly freezing all movement, 'you'll get kicked if you do it like that!' An anxious

59

look came over her and she passed the needle back to me to demonstrate a better technique. The heifer flinched as I squeezed it in, but she kept her feet on the ground, and Heather soon got the idea and completed the series of injections.

'That's just about the most important part of the whole operation,' I said, eliciting a broad smile from my fledgling anaesthetist. 'If you don't do it properly, the cow soon puts the vet and the scalpel on the back wall!' Heather's pleased-with-herself smile turned a bit serious with this realisation, and the two brothers milked her discomfiture with knowing winks.

'Aye,' said Albert sagely, 'ah bet your teachers mek it sound right easy, but when you get down to actually doing it, it'll be a lot harder, ah bet.' We all agreed on this point and I brought the bucket of water into the light ready for the next stage.

'You wash the flank off, Heather, and I'll lay out the instruments while the anaesthetic starts to work. Don't let any dirty water run down over the incision site, remember!'

'He's a fussy bugger is Mr Smith, isn't he, love!' said Hugh, sensing that she needed some moral support. Heather glanced up at me as she lathered the soap, unsure of how she was supposed to answer this loaded question. 'Yes, he is' might have sounded a bit disrespectful, so she settled for 'I expect he has to be, tutoring students like me!' and seemed to enjoy being made to feel part of the team.

While Heather worked away, I opened the pack of sterile surgical instruments and laid them out on the table, their stainless steel glinting in the bright light.

'Finished?' I asked, as she threw another swab of cotton wool into the corner.

'I think that's OK,' she offered, standing back so that I could inspect her effort.

'That looks fine,' I said, not revealing that I'd had my eagle eye on her all the time I'd been preparing the instruments. 'Now, I'll just test the anaesthesia,' I said, and proceeded to prod a needle into the intended incision site. To our relief, the heifer barely moved a muscle. 'Excellent,' I said. 'Right, Heather, give your arms a final scrub up. Hugh, just hold her nose will you – better safe than sorry!'

Nose holding is a time-honoured means of restraining a bovine animal; a finger and thumb in each nostril focuses the mind and diverts attention from any discomfort, just like a twitch for horses or biting the bullet for humans. With hands washed and disinfected, I nonchalantly presented Heather with the scalpel.

'Am I . . . ?' she began, nervously glancing at the heifer, whose eye returned a steady gaze past Hugh's embracing arm. The animal's flank steamed in the floodlight.

'Don't see why not,' I said confidently, 'you'll be qualified and on your own this time next year!' A hush descended and Albert shifted to a better vantage point as Heather turned to the heifer's flank, warm and brightly lit against the shadows on the dusty walls.

'About here?' she asked, threatening an area of skin with the scalpel.

'Just a bit higher,' I indicated, standing alongside her now. She pressed in the blade and started the incision. 'Bit firmer,' I said, 'it takes some cutting through, does leather.' She redoubled her resolve, and slowly and deliberately enlarged the cut downwards.

'Just mind she doesn't kick you, young lady,' said Albert, suddenly feeling a bit fatherly towards her, 'she was quite lively when we were putting t'halter on.'

'It's all right,' I said over my shoulder, 'students don't matter, it's me that should be watching out!' Albert smiled at this age old reference to the dispensibility of veterinary students and rested some more weight on his stick, completely enclosing the knob with his heavy hands. He turned his attention back to the red gash in his heifer's side.

Heather eventually had the skin incision completed and stood back to survey the result. A small artery or two was spraying a fine fountain of blood into the space between us.

'Shall I do the next layer?' I asked tactfully, hoping she wouldn't mind me hurrying things on a bit. Hugh gave me a broad wink while Heather passed me some surgical scissors.

Students see more operations on dogs and cats than on cattle, simply because it's such a regular affair in small animal practice. The difference between the thin flank of a dog and the muscular thickness of a cow's comes as a bit of a shock to them, and it must have looked a bit crude as I worked the scissors up and down, the three layers of muscle twitching involuntarily as their fibres were sliced. A slight hiss of air signalled my entry into the abdominal cavity, and we were soon looking at the shiny surface of the cow's rumen. I stood back and invited Heather to locate the calf.

'You can let go of her nose now,' I said, and Hugh sighed a sigh of relief and shook some circulation back into his fingers. He wiped them across his jumper and folded his arms as he gazed in thinly concealed amazement at the gaping hole in his heifer's flank. The heifer leant back on the halter and stepped away from the wall.

'Whoa, girl,' said Hugh, rapidly leaning into her shoulder to steady her. Heather groped into the depths of the abdomen, trying her arm first in one direction, then another.

'Can I have a commentary?' I asked at length. She sought inspiration from the ceiling again and then announced that she'd found it.

'There'd be trouble if you couldn't!' I joked, passing her the scissors, 'but have you found its head?' I demonstrated that you

didn't need to probe with such delicacy. The calf would weigh a
good thirty-five kilograms, and tracing its outline through the
thick cocooning womb needed a firm hand. I heaved it up from
the depths of the belly, agitating the heifer somewhat as I did
so.

'Whoa, girl,' responded Albert, aware that this was a critical
moment.

'Right,' I said quietly but tersely, 'cut the uterus here.'

Heather reached in with the scissors and opened a way through
to the calf. The heifer thought this would be a good moment to
try a final strain to deliver the calf herself, ballooning the huge
stomach over our arms and emptying some fluid down our boots.

'Not long now,' I said aloud, hoping she wouldn't do that
again. 'Right, same as before, Heather, a generous incision.'

Heather scissored some way along the length of the calf, the
opening womb spilling out more fluid down our calving gowns. I
transferred my grip directly to the calf's leg now and began to
ease it out. The head followed, shiny, smooth and slippery.
Galvanised into action, Albert cast aside his stick, rolled up his
sleeves and made to grab a foot. Farmers were no respecters of the
principles of surgical sterility.

'LEAVE IT TO ME,' I interrupted as we drew it further and
further out, and finally almost collapsed under the weight of this
bundle of new life, slippery as seaweed. 'Right, Albert, *now* you
can have a go,' and he knelt down to clear its nose and mouth
with those work-hardened hands of his.

'Bull,' he said, lifting a back leg, and it responded by blinking
its eye and giving a few rattling coughs. The tension was suddenly
gone. The heifer relaxed and we set to work putting her back
together again.

'I'll stitch the uterus, if you don't mind, 'cause that's a vital bit;
then you can do the rest.'

'OK,' Heather agreed, and passed me a long length of catgut and a large needle. 'You hold the womb up into the wound, and that'll save me a lot of time,' I went on, aware that we must be into the small hours now.

'Do they do cups of tea at High Laithe at this time in a morning?' I asked Hugh.

'I was just going to ask if you wanted a drink yet,' he said with a grin of satisfaction, and, taking another good look at the calf, he ducked out of the doorway and set off for the farm kitchen. I stitched up the uterus, emphasising some important points to Heather as I did so, and then set her up stitching the flank together again.

The tea duly arrived on a tray, but much of its heat had not survived the journey across the farmyard. Still, it was warm and wet, as they say, and I was able to drink it with one hand while giving Heather a bit of assistance with the other. Long lengths of catgut have an annoying habit of tangling themselves round anything which presents itself, hindering what should be a simple, repetitive procedure.

As soon as she finished, I grabbed a new needle and some stout nylon thread, telling her to drink her now lukewarm tea while I started on the skin. It takes a bit of dexterity to work the heavy needle-holders necessary to force thread through cowhide, but after emptying her mug, Heather soon got the hang of it and took over again to finish the last few stitches, matching the ones I had placed.

'That looks better,' said Hugh with relief. 'It takes longer to sew up than to do the operation itself.'

'It is a bit of a bore,' I said, 'but worth it if you've got a live calf looking at you.'

'Aye – it'd never 'ave come out alive proper way,' rejoined Albert. 'Just look at the size o' them hips.' The calf was already

LET YOUR LIGHT SHINE

trying to find its feet, and mother, still haltered, was getting agitated and feeling a frustration of her instincts.

'Give her a double dose of penicillin, Heather, and then we can let her go. We'll come and take the stitches out in ten days,' I said to the brothers, 'but if she's not eating and healthy in the meantime, get on the phone sooner rather than later. Got that?' I added, to reinforce the point. 'We don't want all this time and money wasted if she gets peritonitis, do we?'

'Ah thowt tha'd be payin' *us*,' said Albert with a glint in his eye, 'seeing as 'ow a student did all the hard work!' Heather smiled and accepted the compliment gratefully. We switched off the big light and felt a glow of satisfaction as mother and calf got to know each other face to face. A few contented lowing noises amidst a vigorous licking suggested that all the trauma had been forgotten.

The night air was cold on our skin, not properly dried on the rough scrap of towel, but we soon had all the gear tidied back into the Land Rover. Hugh Clarkson stood in the doorway, silhouetted against the glow in the old building.

'Thanks very much,' he called, 'that's b'in a grand job. Goodnight to you!'

While we drove off into the night and back to bed, he and Albert would be staying up to make sure the calf got its first feed.

On Reflection

Heather went on to pass her finals with flying colours, and is now an assistant in a busy practice, combining some farm animal work with helping to run a branch practice with its morning and evening surgeries. We hear through the grapevine that she is establishing a good reputation for herself, and it is gratifying to know that our practice contributed something towards her long training. No doubt she will soon find herself assisting the next generation of veterinary surgeons who come to her practice as students.

A few undergraduates are overconfident and 'too cocky by half'. They usually find themselves 'pulled down a peg or two' as they go through the mill of a university course, steered that way by discerning tutors or well-meaning fellow-students! The majority, however, need to gain confidence in using their knowledge and applying practical skills on real animals. Dogs and cats, horses and cows are all quick to take advantage of the situation if they suspect their consultant is at all tentative, hesitant or insecure. (Sheep aren't usually that analytical!)

Trust and confidence are also the building blocks of human relationships, whether at work, in friendships or in the family. Once lost, they are exceedingly difficult to rebuild and the strength of that relationship suffers, usually very significantly.

Trust and confidence are, of course, an essential part of Christian faith, trust and confidence in a God whom we 'exalt above the heavens', as one of the psalms says. i.e. miles beyond the reach of all foreseeable space-rockets or galactic probes. As Jesus said to doubting Thomas, 'blessed are those who have *not seen* and yet have believed.' (Jn. 20:29) (My italics).

'And yet have believed.' Becoming a believer in Jesus Christ is usually a turning point in someone's life, but a confidence in God, laced with humility, is part of the fulfilment and growth of that belief or faith. How did the father greet the prodigal son when he had come to that turning point? By going out to meet him, throwing his arms round him and kissing him. How confident did the poor lad feel? 'I am no longer worthy to be called your son,' was all he could find to say. (Luke 15:21) Presumably, after the feast and celebration, he felt the foundations of a new and lasting relationship. Trust and confidence were being rebuilt.

LET YOUR LIGHT SHINE

A quietly growing confidence is a great blessing, helping us to pray fervently, helping us to persevere with difficult passages in the Bible and, at the deepest level, helping us to stay on a more even keel when we meet everyday trials and tribulations. Just before his death, Jesus said, 'Peace I leave with you, my peace I give you.' His peace, remember, had him sound asleep in the back of the boat when his disciples were terrified that they were about to sink! (Mark 4:38)

In the same way that Heather's confidence grew with practice (if you'll excuse the pun!) so a person's faith grows in confidence as they spend time with other Christians in the presence of the Lord, time in private prayer, and time in reading and reflecting on passages, or even just phrases of scripture. Many people find that committing a few words to memory is an invaluable help for those occasions when we just can't get to sleep. Allowing the words to turn slowly over in the mind soon brings calm, and something of God enters our very soul, building an inner confidence and peace.

St. Paul had the most arduous of lives when he became an apostle, almost never out of trouble or hardship. He travelled great distances, was shipwrecked, beaten up and imprisoned on more than one occasion, but could still say that 'the peace of God, which transcends all understanding will guard your hearts and your minds in Christ Jesus.' (Phil. 4:7) That was no confidence trick. That was reality. May we all attain some measure of a similar confidence in Almighty God.

CHAPTER SEVEN

A Free Gift

VISIT ANY TOURIST information office and you will see what a virtue is made of the local countryside, its produce and its buildings. It seems that we have a need to reassure ourselves of our farming roots, in spite of the fact that most of us now live in or near towns and cities which we zoom between along trunk roads and motorways.

Although that's the reality, however, we instinctively want to overlay reality with nostalgic notions of working horses, a village sized scale of life and a timeless pattern of human activities. We like to contrast frantic scenes in the stockmarket (as seen on TV), with its representation of all that is highly technological, fast, flashy, lucrative, yet highly stressful – we like to contrast that with mental images of rural vistas, old country churches in old country villages where people gather outside the pub in summer to linger and chat under an old oak tree. We imagine there a tranquillity in the pace of life and in the very stonework of walls and buildings, a tranquillity which we sometimes envy and reach out for, to capture a little into our own lives.

The fact is, though, that the countryside and agriculture are changing along with everything else. Nowadays, not many farmyards boast a manure heap, gently steaming on frosty mornings; it's called slurry now and is kept in huge tanks, later to be splattered over the land like cold porridge. The hens and

ducks and geese have mostly gone, either gone for good or gone into intensive production inside controlled-environment houses. The simple tractors which once displaced the heavy horses have themselves now been overshadowed by gently growling four-wheel-drive monsters with air-conditioned cabs and quadra-phonic radio! The familiar clatter of milking machine buckets as they used to be lugged around on the dairy floor has been replaced by the soft hiss of escaping air as milk glides and pulses along glass pipework, direct from cow to stainless steel cooling tank. All this change represents progress of course, but it is mildly worrying that speakers at agricultural conferences no longer refer to farms as farms, but prefer instead the word 'unit'. This seems to have removed any sense of individuality, or the link between a farm's acres, its soil and its past. You certainly won't find any 'units' mentioned in the Doomsday Book, but only farms with names which give a clue to their identity – Manor Farm, Church Farm, Moorend Farm or Dalehead Farm for instance.

Despite this trend, however, it never ceases to amaze me how wide is the generation and culture gap between individual farms and farmers. While some are close behind the leading edge of agricultural technology, pushed ever onwards by research institutions, trial farms and agricultural scientists, yet others seem to have changed little since the early nineteen sixties. Although these farmers have fallen behind the times in many ways, and their children have grown up with no desire to pursue a farming life, yet they make a welcome contrast and relief from the pressures of time and economics which we live with on the very up-to-date 'units'.

Duncan Sutcliffe and his wife Cynthia were one couple who perfectly illustrated this reluctance to change a system which actually didn't need changing. Change means new investment, and when you've worked hard all your lives, as they had, then a new bank loan is a prospect to be avoided if at all possible.

Oxleaze Farm was reached by a long track incorporating two wooden gates which, when livestock were out, had to be opened and shut as you drove in and out of the place. Cattle grids weren't a high priority on Duncan's job list. The yard, although mostly concreted, was always rather dirty as various groups of hens, ducks, guinea fowl and peacocks left mucky footprints and droppings across the surface. The calf rearing building, with its flagstone floors and low doorway, remained exactly as it had been built more than a century beforehand and the milk cows were still tethered in the time honoured way in a cowshed, or shippon as the local term is. The only concession you could find to any new development was the new shippon built in the mid eighties – an exact replica of the original! These two shippons were still mucked out twice daily by brush and shovel, and one had to admire the way Duncan and his ilk could brush the floor under a cow's back feet and deftly propel the accumulated excreta along the passage, regularly cleaning off the bristles with a double stamping of the brush head upon the floor. The cornered mass would then be shovelled into the waiting barrow, wooden of course, and wheeled across the yard to the midden or muckspreader.

Having climbed far enough up the farming ladder to satisfy his personal ambition, Duncan felt in a position to survey the farming scene not from a pinnacle of achievement but from the point of view of someone who had lived long enough to realise that there was nothing new under the sun, and accordingly took a fairly relaxed view of life, punctuated, it has to be said, by reasonably frequent crises, usually of his own making. His innate good humour, and fondness of making jokes and sarcastic comments at the vet's expense, was part of his nature, and he was constantly alert for an opportunity to embarrass, tease or shame – the cost of veterinary services being a most fertile source of such quips. His name came up one morning as we gathered in the farm office to sort out our rounds.

'It's Duncan Sutcliffe for you,' said Pauline, handing me the phone, 'something about a cow with a thick hock.'

'Morning, Duncan,' I said cheerfully, 'how are you today?'

'Well,' he said, with a slight chuckle, 'poor – but hearty! Ha, ha!' He laughed at his own witticism, but anxious not to get involved in economic discussions over the phone, I steered the conversation back to the matter in hand. Regaining a more serious tone, he explained, 'Your assistant gave me some injections last week but they don't seem to have helped mi' cow any. I'd really like you or Roger to come and have a look – she's still terrible swollen about the hock an' 'ardly giving any milk at all now.'

'I'm coming out your way this morning so I'll have a look at it,' I said, writing his name in the day book as I spoke.

'Does that mean it'll be a free visit?' replied Duncan, his wide smile being apparent over the telephone as he scored his first point.

'No,' I replied as quick as a flash, 'you'll get charged as usual – it's the other fellow who'll get the free visit!' I was pleased by my counter thrust and the shocked intake of breath it produced from my client but, assuring him of my best attention, I put the phone down with a smile and completed the daybook entry: 'Sutcliffe, Oxleaze Farm – cow thick hock,' and appended my initials in the margin.

My first two calls involved quite a lot of work, so it was nearly half-past eleven before I arrived at Duncan's, wiping my brow theatrically as I slid out of the driver's seat and started to pull my boots on. Duncan was leaning back against the wall, resting on a long shepherd's crook and studying me through his glasses. 'What's all this in aid of?' he asked, wiping a dirty sleeve across his own forehead.

'I was wondering if there might be a cup of tea available,' I said, adding, 'I haven't had a drink since before breakfast,' in the hope that I might elicit some sympathy.

'Cup of tea?' he echoed, in mock surprise, apparently shocked that such a matter should be raised when there was work to be done.

'I thought it might lubricate the old brain cells a bit,' I offered, hoping he would see the sense of employing a brain that was fully engaged.

He raised his deerstalker to scratch his head and replied querulously, 'I'll see what I can do,' and he started off towards the farmhouse. By the time I had got myself ready, he returned with the information that Cynthia was 'dropping everything' to put the kettle on for me.

Offering suitable expressions of gratitude, I stepped across to the shippon door and waited for Duncan to show me the cow. The long line of cows all stood up in their stalls as they sensed the presence of a stranger, but the animal I was to look at was the exception, quite content to remain on the floor. We accosted her with various nudges and noises, but whereas most cows would have responded immediately, this one barely glanced at us. The reason was not difficult to see. The hock is the angular joint half way down an animal's back leg and on this cow, it was nearly twice the normal size, with the outside surface having lost its hair on account of the pressure within it. On cupping my hands gently around it, I could sense the heat and appreciate the pain and swelling, but I needed to see her standing up to make a proper assessment. Concrete cowsheds soon acquire polished floors from the constant wear: great if you're a dairy hygiene inspector looking for sluiced down surfaces which harbour no dirt, but not so great if you're a heavy bovine animal that needs to lie down for long periods, resting and cudding.

With some more vigorous coercion, we were at last able to provoke a response from the cow and with an almost visible grimace, she struggled to her feet but I was pleased to see that she could at least bear some weight on the affected limb.

I studied the hock for some time and from different angles, mentally rehearsing the different treatments which had been advocated. Like many farmers, Duncan, having constant contact with his animals, quite literally so at milking times, had failed to notice the growing seriousness of the cow's problem, and, catching my mood, his normally cheerful disposition gave way to a very anxious expression. Keen to break the tension, he reached for a bottle from the dusty windowsill.

'This is what Malcolm put up for me,' he said, thrusting it under my nose, and then withdrawing to await my considered opinion. I read the label, noting that Malcolm had prescribed an antibiotic, and turned to the cow again.

'You're not going to say it's hopeless, are you?' said Duncan, a rising tone matching his growing concern.

'You know as well as I do,' I said, 'that this isn't just your average thick hock. Occasionally they do become hopeless cases but that's very rare. Nevertheless, we need to be very determined if we're going to give her a decent chance of a quick recovery.'

Duncan breathed a sigh of relief, but then alerted himself to the possible implications of a 'determined' course of treatment. 'Will it be expensive?' he asked, a sudden wave of pain widening his pupils.

'It'll be more expensive in time than in money,' I answered. 'It needs an intensive regime of hot poulticing to disperse that swelling or, if possible, to make it burst and drain the infection.'

'Oh – we can cope with that,' said Duncan, congeniality flooding his face once more, 'I thought you were going to advise some fancy-priced injections!'

'No,' I continued in my best professional manner, 'she'll just need some anti-inflammatory powders to drench her with, but there is one more thing. I want you to get one of those rubber cow mats for her to lie on, otherwise, your bathing will be helping the cow but the hard concrete will be hindering any recovery.' Rubber cow mats are a fairly recent innovation designed to satisfy the dairy hygiene inspector with a nice clean surface while the cow has a bed of much greater comfort. The only trouble is, they're expensive.

'I don't know about that,' said Duncan, scratching the back of his head, 'are you sure she can't make do with a bit more sawdust as bedding?'

'Dead sure,' I answered, making the point as definitely as I could, but glad to have the tension broken as Cynthia shouted from outside that tea was served. We left the cowshed and gratefully seized the large mugs of tea which she proffered on a tin tray. 'How's that for good service?' she asked with a fulsome smile.

'Absolutely marvellous, Mrs Sutcliffe,' I said, 'and never more welcome!'

'Ah, biscuits as well today!' Duncan interrupted, selecting one with big grimy fingers and winking at the easy rapport which had grown up over the years between his wife and the vet. Through a mouthful of crumbs, he added, 'Of course, I shall expect a suitable deduction from the bill!' at which he grinned hugely, rocking backwards on one foot and waving half an oatcake in my direction. I took another drink of tea and asked his wife if she had enjoyed the concert last week.

'Wonderful,' she replied, 'we're very fortunate to be able to hear such music in a little town like Colston, aren't we?'

'We are indeed,' I agreed, reaching into the back of the Land Rover and handing Duncan a packet of powders. 'Give your cow one a day as a drench,' I instructed him.

'Do I get a refund on those antibiotics,' he chipped in, 'seeing as how they didn't do any good?'

'I'll be back in a week to see how she's getting on,' I continued dryly, but with just a hint of a glint in my eye.

'Have another biscuit,' Cynthia said, nodding at the tea tray and smiling . . .

During the next few days, I had occasion to visit Stephen and Jane Barker at Briarbank Farm in order to carry out pregnancy diagnoses and infertility checks on some of their cows. Stephen and Jane were in their early thirties, and as well as building up a family of four fine boys, they had also built up a herd of a hundred and twenty-five pedigree dairy cows where there had once been just an outbarn. Through sheer hard work, and the backing of their farming parents, they had built first the cattle yards, cubicles and milking parlour, and finally, the farmhouse. Not bad on a hilltop site in the Pennines.

On this particular day, Stephen was making use of the school holidays to allow the boys to help with the cows when the vet came, and how eager and excited they were to be involved in real work. Nice people as they were, however, Stephen and Jane were not the sort of people who would tolerate any nonsense, either from the cows or the children! At Briarbank, the cows were milked three times a day instead of the usual two, and with so much work to get through every day, they couldn't afford anything or anybody to get out of line. The great advantage to the practice, however, was that the animals to be seen were always separated out, ready for the vet, and there was never any question of there being a 'first find your cow' situation.

On this occasion, I had to use our mobile scanner to determine which cows had conceived and which were still empty. As we ushered the first five cows into the stalls built for the purpose, Jane looked on with motherly satisfaction as the boys identified each cow, and read off from a clipboard the date when each had been inseminated. With such an enthusiastic band of helpers, I took great pleasure in showing them the embryo calves, approximately six weeks old now, on the scanner screen, and wide-eyed was their delight when they could locate the tiny heartbeat and put another tick across that cow's number.

After nearly an hour of this, we were getting the last batch in as Jane said to call at the house for a drink. 'I'll have a cheque ready for you as well,' she grinned, as though any more incentive were needed!

Chats over the kitchen table were never a waste of time, but rather, a good opportunity to exchange agricultural news and to keep a finger on the pulse of the client, both family and farm. Stephen and Jane needed little encouragement from me to explain how the results of my work would be typed into the farm computer where each cow's record was kept, and from which all the herd forecasts and action lists would be made. I had noticed some shiny new stainless steel dials in the parlour, and they responded to my interest, explaining how each cow had its milk yield automatically recorded on computer disc. This information was in turn used to ration exactly how much extra concentrate feed each cow received – extra that is to the vast mountain of grass silage stored in the huge new building and sliced off each day in large chunks by a tractor-mounted grab. You could sense how the whole family was involved as the elder boys chipped in with their own enthusiastic contributions. Time was pressing for all of us, however, and with no time for a second cup, I made some jovial comment to the boys and took my leave. As I drove down the steep track, I mused that although we might practise in what the Brussels bureaucrats called a 'less favourable area' and several practices in the county had become pet only establishments, nevertheless, with clients like the Barkers, we had some hope for the future of our farm animal work.

Suffused with such comfortable thoughts, I arrived back at the surgery to find that meanwhile, Duncan Sutcliffe had phoned in with a message. It read, 'Mr Smith needn't come and look at cow tomorrow – bit better.' I let out a sigh of frustration at Duncan's latest economy. I could understand his thrifty approach to our professional services (his neighbour once confided that he'd 'split a halfpenny narrow way', would Duncan) but it was his economy of words which really needled me. My concern for his cow, and my intention to persist with it until it was better, was repaid with the superficial clinical report – 'bit better.' I would have liked to know so much more detail: had it softened? – had it burst? – was she taking any more weight on it? I made a mental note to call next time I went past his farm.

As it happened, however, Duncan had occasion to phone up the very next Saturday evening. He had a sheep to lamb and it was my weekend on duty. It was a filthy night, pitch black under the unseen blanket of cloud, and raining heavily. I put all my waterproofs on at home to avoid getting soaked in his yard, and so arrived ready for action. 'It's in the old hen house,' said Duncan, looking over his misted spectacles as the rain ran down his ruddy cheeks. 'Have you got a torch?' We trudged across the dimly lit yard, turning our collars up tight against our necks, but had to cross a sea of mud and then duck under a fence to get to the old wooden hen-house. Shaking the water off our coats, we picked out the ewe in the torch beam and managed to corner her. Duncan produced a small bucket of lukewarm water containing a disintegrating block of soap – no doubt the same water he'd used to examine his ewe forty minutes earlier! The floor was deep litter – several years worth of it, in fact – but if not the latest in obstetrical hygiene, at least it was dry and soft to kneel on.

Duncan held the sheep with one hand while he rather unhelpfully shone the torch in my face with the other. I washed her off and gently inserted my hand, soon identifying the condition known as 'ring-womb'. The neck of the womb starts to soften and relax as normal, but then the process halts, long before there's space enough for the birth of the lamb.

'It's tight, isn't it?' said the farmer, anxious for me to confirm that it was still constricted and my visit was definitely not an unnecessary one.

'Yes, it is,' I replied into the torchlight, thinking at the same time of an obvious, but unmentionable, connection between patient and client! After a few more seconds' investigation, I decided that with a little patience, I would be able to dilate the cervix to allow a normal birth.

'It's so tight, Duncan,' I said confidently, 'so irreducibly tight, that I shall have to do a Caesarian operation.'

The torch beam jerked up towards the roof trusses as my client flinched at this turn of the screw, and then painfully repeated – 'A Caesarian . . . how much will that cost?'

'I'm not exactly sure what the figure is,' I replied, 'but quite a few pounds I suppose. We should get a live lamb though,' I added encouragingly.

All the while, I secretly continued to spread my fingers inside the ewe as poor Duncan braced himself against the financial shockwaves which now threatened his composure. There followed a motionless pause when all went quiet in the old hen-house. Outside, water dripped from the gutterless roof until at length, he could contain himself no longer.

'Couldn't you give it some sort of relaxing injection,' he almost pleaded, adding, 'sometimes they just need a bit more time.' I returned my reply along the torchbeam. 'That would merely postpone the inevitable, Duncan,' I said, 'and the lamb might not live that long.'

'Mi' Dad always used to give them a calcium injection – that seemed to help sometimes,' he countered. He was clutching at straws now, but my mental cruelty had to have a limit and in any case, my silently working fingers were opening up the ring-womb very nicely now. I introduced this new development into our dialogue. 'Hang on a minute, Duncan, I think there's a bit of softening here . . . yes – I can get two legs and a nose!'

If ever will-power could effect the delivery of a lamb, then Duncan Sutcliffe was at that moment doing his best to demonstrate it. I glanced at his facial contortion in the dimly reflected lamplight as I eased the lamb's body into the ever softening cervix.

'That's amazing,' I breathed as the lamb slithered onto the earthen floor and blinked up at Duncan, who disbelievingly leant forwards to bathe it in light. It coughed its first breath and Duncan retreated and relaxed, releasing a sigh of relief.

'You had me worried there, vet,' he confessed, wiping the damp from his brow, 'how did you do it?'

'Pure skill, Duncan,' I said, reaching into the ewe again for a post-natal check. Sure enough, there was another lamb and within a few seconds, I had it sliding onto its twin. 'Would you like two for the price of one?' I said, gesturing at the gasping pair.

'Well, I'll go to heck,' he said, bending forward to see for himself. 'Well, I never,' he continued, regaining a standing position, 'I never thought she was going to have no more than one this time!'

We spent a few more moments putting the ewe back on her feet and introducing her to her offspring, and then gathered up our things to leave her in the dark hen-house, engrossed in licking them into life.

We arrived back at the farmyard and I dodged into the shippon door with Duncan hard on my heels. 'What's all this about?' he asked, switching the light on and disturbing all the cows.

'I just remembered that cow – thought I'd cast my eye over it,' I answered, striding down the causeway to the animal in question. To my great satisfaction, she was already getting to her feet and proceeded to stretch her back and lift her tail.

'There's always a barrowload more muck when the vet comes,' Duncan grumbled, reaching for the shovel.

While he tidied the steaming pile away, I noted how the pain had gone out of the cow's face and how she was standing four-square now. True, the hock was still enlarged and a bead of pus was emerging from a small hole, but I could handle the joint with little sign of discomfort now. 'What happened to the rubber mat, Duncan?' I asked.

'Been a bit too busy to go and get one,' he replied lamely, 'but it's a lot better, isn't it?'

'Yes,' I said, 'you've been doing a good job with the bathing – keep it up till there's no more pus showing.' I paused at the shippon door to wash my boots at the corner tap, but realised my mistake too late as Duncan leant his back against the door.

'I was thinking about mi' sheep,' he began. 'Will it be a freebie tonight,' he asked, 'seeing as 'ow you thought it was going to be an operation job an' nearly gave the farmer a heart attack?'

I registered the expectant look in his face as I turned off the tap. 'I think my partner would say that in view of the skill involved, the difficult circumstances, and bearing in mind the delivery of two live lambs, we should properly make double the normal charge. Give my regards to the wife,' I added cheerfully as

I edged past him to pull on the iron door handle. I retreated across the shiny yard, leaving the mortified figure of Duncan Sutcliffe silhouetted in the doorway, stammering incoherently as he tried in vain for a suitable rejoinder.

On Reflection

While Duncan was a traditionalist in many ways, he was bang up to date when it came to expecting 'freebies'. Like all of us, he was very aware of the free gifts offered with petrol tokens, free credit on his wife's new washing machine, or a free wax jacket if he put all his insurance in the hands of a certain office.

If that is the way of the world, can we approach God with the same attitude and expectation? Free gifts are so abundant in the business world and shopping precinct that we might easily allow the concept to colour our thinking in other areas of life. Perhaps it's a good thing to remind ourselves of the first commandment, that we should approach God with our wholehearted love, employing all our heart and soul, all our mind and strength. We can worship him as our creator and thank him for all the blessings of this life, but it doesn't end there for, as George Carter exclaimed at the beginning, 'Our God is a very gracious God!' Giving is part of his nature!

I remember the time when I was searching for a new reality in my Christian faith, a faith I could call my own, not just an inherited tradition which had little meaning for me. In looking for something to fill this emptiness, I was astounded to come across the words of Jesus – 'Whoever believes in me . . . streams of living water will flow from within him.' (Jn. 7:38) Flow *from*! I was bemused for a long time because I was wanting it to read 'flow *into*'! I hadn't yet understood about God wanting me to open my heart to him so that he could place a stepping stone there, from which to influence my whole being. Only then could there be any chance of living waters flowing out!

I discovered of course, that the transaction was completely free! God was keeping his promise:

Come, all you who are thirsty, come to the waters;
and you who have no money, come buy and eat!
Come buy wine and milk without money and without cost.

(Is. 55:1)

Now isn't just the sort of freebie that Duncan would have leapt at?

For the Christian, that promise finds its fulfilment in Jesus whom, guess what, God gave to us in the first place and for all eternity. Perhaps this is why the most famous verse in the Bible is Jn. 3:16: 'For God so loved the world that he *gave* his one and only Son, that whoever believes in him shall not perish but have everlasting life.'

During his ministry on earth, Jesus was a living demonstration of the kingdom of heaven, but mankind rejected God's gift and Jesus was put to death. The night before he died, however, he was concerned with another demonstration. At the last supper with his disciples, he took some bread, gave thanks, broke it, handed it to them and said, 'This is my body given for you...' (Luke 22:19) Another act of giving. Every time we take communion and reflect on these words, it's humbling to consider just what we are receiving. We also do well to remember that we are to be channels of God's gifts, with a responsibility to others. As Jesus told the twelve disciples when he sent them out to preach the gospel:

'Freely you have received, freely give.' (Matt. 10:8)

CHAPTER EIGHT

No Lame Excuses

I HATE PAIN AND SUFFERING. They get into my soul. Professional involvement, however, usually overrides inner emotions and a slight clenching of my jaw was all that Jonathan Hargreaves might have noticed as he urged his cow across the yard into a small pen. One gets used to seeing lame animals, but this one was really suffering. It wasn't just limping, it simply couldn't bear to put its foot anywhere near the ground and consequently had a most awkward, three-legged gait. The offending foot must have been a source of searing pain which lanced up the whole limb, completely dominating the small brain of its owner, a black and white dairy cow.

With a few desperate steps at a time, Mr Hargreaves coaxed his cow into the pen and together, we persuaded her into the cattle crush, a tubular steel frame with a wooden floor. The name 'crush' is very inappropriate as the cow hardly touches the sides, but it does restrain her and allows her feet to be lifted one by one and trimmed safely. Jonathan was a good stockman and usually called us in good time when one of his animals needed our attention. He must have been reading my thoughts as he quickly explained that it was one of his late calvers.

'I've had it summering with a batch of heifers up Bleasdale,' he said. 'T'chap up there reckons to look 'em for me; I only go up there once a week or so. I don't know how he missed this 'cause it

85

was gay lame when I went up on Saturday. If he'd bothered to phone me, he'd have saved me coming all the way back for the trailer.'

As I attached the lifting strap to the cow's leg, Jonathan explained how he'd returned up the dale with his wife Suzanne, just managing to load her (the cow!) 'at the edge o'dark'. 'We tried to have a look ourselves yesterday, but she won't let you near it, it's so sensitive.'

Sure enough, as soon as we winched the leg up, she started crashing about in pain and we lowered her leg again quickly before she injured herself, or us. Before trying again, I gave her a dose of sedative and prepared a syringeful of local anaesthetic. I was relieved to find that, as we hoisted her leg up for a second time, she could just about stand still long enough to allow me to find the vein and inject the local without battering me. It made my hands tremble, but as Jonathan had discovered, treatment of this foot was only by kind permission of its owner!

As the anaesthetic began to work, the foot became as numb as a piece of melon, and my confidence grew as the cow relaxed, free of that awful pain for the first time in days. I got to work, scrubbing off the dirt and then removing slices of hoof, looking for tell-tale marks in the fresh surface. I soon found the blackening I was looking for, right at the toe, and slicing more deeply now, was rewarded by a few drips of black pus and a characteristically disgusting smell. Tracing the abscess more deeply, I found that it had tracked under the wall of the hoof, splitting it in the process and . . . well, we all know the pain of a split nail; imagine the pain if matter was weeping out of that split and you were trying to walk on it!

'She wouldn't have let me do that,' said Jonathan, examining the foot while I reached for a different hoof knife, 'not a cat in hell's chance!'

'I was dead lucky getting that local in,' I said, allowing a sense of success to wash away the tension. 'You can't hope to do a job like this without good anaesthesia.'

I had to bend over and squint to open out that split up the front wall of the hoof, awkwardly upside down with the leg held in this position. I was perspiring freely now as the heat from the cow, the summer sun on my back and the energy of working, all sent my core temperature soaring. At last I had the job done, we washed the split clean and encased the foot in cotton wool and bandage.

'You'll have maggots in there if you're not careful,' I warned as we finally lowered the foot to the floor. 'Remove the bandage every two or three days and soak the foot in a bucket of salty water. Then you can put a clean dressing on.'

Suzanne appeared with two mugs of tea at that point and the world felt very good as the cow backed out of the crush, walking normally and looking – well, if not grateful, at least quite content.

'I bet that feels better,' said Jonathan, 'do you think the calf will be all right? She shouldn't be due for another month or so.'

'The calf will be fine,' I said with conviction, 'but don't forget, the anaesthetic's still working so the foot'll be sore again in an hour or so.'

Nothing could remove Jonathan's satisfied smile, however. 'I have every confidence she's over the worst now,' he said.

Although that was a particularly bad case, lameness of a more sinister nature has been a real problem in cattle over the last twenty-five or thirty years. Get stuck in the car on a summer afternoon behind a herd of cows going to be milked and you'll more than likely see an example of what I mean. The leading cows will be setting the pace, creatures of habit, looking forward to being milked and sure of the way home. Bringing up the rear, cajoled by a person with dog, stick or quad-bike, will be one or more cows struggling to keep up because they are lame. Not walking with a pronounced limp, but with a more subtle, shuffling gait because they have probably got not one lame foot, but two painful back feet. A gait which screams in agony to the trained observer – the equivalent of walking in a pair of badly fitting leather boots which over the months have caused corns, blisters, bruising, infection and necrosis.

Lameness in dairy cows is one of the scandals of the industry, a cause of severe economic loss and a national disgrace. We see it nearly every day. We see lame horses almost every day too – competition horses which are out of work because of a limp, usually only detectable at the trot or canter. Most horses like this are quite happy to have a few days rest in a stable or paddock while the problem resolves. Lame dairy cows, on the other hand, suffer more or less constant pain, only relieved by lying down. They walk out of the milking parlour in pain, walk to the pasture or winter feed area in pain and lie down again as soon as possible. When they try to stand up again, they have another pain barrier to go through, and often make very clumsy attempts, regaining their feet only after a considerable struggle. Not surprisingly, they soon lose weight, and start to look dirty and scruffy-coated. Horses receive expert attention from the farrier every six or eight weeks. The horse is trained to pick each foot up in turn and rest it on the farrier's lap while he 'dresses' the foot and replaces the shoe. Cows, on the other hand, rarely receive attention to their feet until they become overgrown or lame. Without specialised equipment, they can be very uncooperative and the farmer or vet is quite likely to get bruised, dirty and heated for his trouble. By virtue of their long training, farriers are experts, and their expertise shows in their workmanship. In contrast, most farmers who purport to treat their own cows have had no formal training and even in veterinary colleges, there simply isn't enough curriculum time to teach the subject thoroughly to students.

The lame cow then, has two problems. First, it's easier for the hard-working farmer to come up with a much more urgent problem, promising the cow that he'll deal with her 'tomorrow'. Second, when he does get round to looking at her foot, its treatment will probably be less than professional. Good enough to improve the lameness, but not a real cure.

'Blimey, that packs a punch, Anthony – I hope you're not a glue sniffer! Makes you high from where *I'm* standing, that stuff does!' I was now up at Steve Mason's farm for a morning trimming cows' feet. The practice owned a proper foot trimming crush which we towed onto farms whenever more than one or two cows needed attention. Thanks to the enormous strides (if you'll excuse the pun) which have been made since the seventies in the treatment of lameness, the once notoriously hard and dirty work was now compensated for by the rewarding results.

'Ugh,' choked Steven. 'It fair makes your eyes water!' he added, wiping his face on his sleeve as I continued to mix the glue. I had pared out a nasty ulcer from the sole of this particular cow, carefully cutting away the ragged edges of hoof to reveal a raw area of quick – dirty, infected and very sore. Being a cloven hoofed animal, however, I could glue a plastic sole onto the unaffected hoof of the foot. This would then take all the weight and so allow the diseased hoof to rest and heal without causing too much more pain. Without having time to look up, I said urgently, 'Quick, Steve, hold that block while I put the glue on – mind your fingers!' These modern adhesives heated up and set very quickly once they had been mixed, so there was no time to lose before facing it up to the cow's foot, the excess resin oozing out round the edges like a squashed egg sandwich.

'Stand still you —,' I said, addressing my patient as she chose this critical moment to try to wave her leg about. We soon relaxed as she steadied again, the glue hardened and within a few minutes, set like flint. We released the ratchet, lowered the leg and opened the door of the crush, allowing the cow to walk out and rejoin her mates.

'That's smashing,' said Steve, with satisfaction written all across his face. 'She'll be filling her bag again in the morning. It's marvellous what you chaps can do!'

He was referring to the fact that, released from pain and impediment, the cow would be eating more heartily and producing more milk within just a day or two, filling her udder properly between milkings. Satisfying work, and gratifying that the farmer gave us the credit. You could say we got a real kick out of it! As Steve opened the gates back into the main yard, I started thankfully to pack up my tackle – knives, shears, cotton wool, syringes, record sheet . . .

'Have you got time for one more?' came a hesitant voice, 'I've just seen one holding a front leg up – it was OK last night.'

'Oh, come on,' I exclaimed testily, 'you said five cows on the phone, we've done seven already and now this!' I grumbled a bit more about it being my half day and it was already quarter to one.

'Will you be in bother with the wife?' grinned Stephen. 'You can come back tomorrow if you're in a hurry.' It was a common dilemma. Do it now while all the equipment was set up, or come back in the morning and spend an inordinate amount of time travelling and reorganising. Steve's big smile and twinkling eyes gave me no option.

'Come on, then,' I said, 'Let's have a quick look.'

Stephen obliged by singling the cow out very quickly, and as she hobbled towards the crush, I had to admit that I couldn't in all conscience have turned my back on her. I had an imaginary conversation with my partner, Roger, as we fitted the supporting straps around her. 'How is it,' I asked him, 'that farmers consistently book in *x* number of jobs and by the time you've finished, there are about three extra?!' We fastened a rope round the cow's lame leg as I invented Roger's reply in my mind. 'It's because they've no concept of time,' he said, 'and they think we've finished for the day when we leave their farms!'

We cleaned off the foot and I pared off the surface layer of hoof, revealing to my great joy that she had nothing more than 'foul-in-the-foot', once a common cause of lameness but now displaced by more difficult conditions. 'You're lucky,' I joked to Stephen, 'all she needs is a quick antibiotic injection and she'll be right in no time.'

'How d'you mean "*I'm* lucky",' he jested, 'it's *you* that's lucky – you'll get your half day after all. Think of us poor farmers – never-ending jobs to do!'

We soon had the crush hosed off and loaded back on the trailer and now it bounced along behind me as I drove out of his yard and headed for home across the moors. I was a little late, yes, but well content with my work and looking forward to a refreshing shower. I hoped 'the wife' had dinner ready as I had worked up a healthy appetite.

Within minutes of arriving back home, I had jettisoned my work clothes and showered, and was soon tucking into my soup and bread. Farmers often joked that if you got home late for a meal, it would be 'hot tongue and cold shoulder' from 'the wife', but the ladies I knew who were married to livestock farming were models of patience and understanding. Wendy, too, had developed a very phlegmatic attitude and kept an attractive table, even when I was late in.

'I'll bring you a cup of tea into the sitting room, if you like,' she said as I gathered up the last crumbs. 'The paper's on the coffee table.' I needed no second bidding and soon relaxed into an armchair, felt the sun on my face and closed my eyes. Bliss . . . comfort . . . oblivion . . .

The cup rattled on the saucer as it was placed on the table in front of me, jerking me back to life. 'How would you feel like a trip to Carlthwaite,' she began, 'there's some shopping I want to do and you need a pair of new shoes.' I choked on the first sip of steaming hot tea, and as I hurriedly wiped my lips heard her continue, 'We could pick up your coat that you said you'd left at the Atkinsons' . . .

'Sure we can,' I answered sweetly, opening up the paper. 'Now,' I thought, 'I wonder if there are any vacancies for a lady diplomat . . . ?'

It was some weeks later before I was on the Hargreaves' farm again, this time to 'vet' half-a-dozen cows – meaning to see if they were in calf or not. As each cow was yoked in the crush, I lubricated my arm and slid it into the cow's rectum through which the womb could be felt, hopefully with a calf inside it.

'About three months for this one,' I said.

'That'll do,' said Jonathan, and the next cow was persuaded into the crush.

After a few minutes, we had done all the six, and found five to be in various stages of pregnancy, the odd one out being empty, or barren as it was known. 'Not to worry,' said Jonathan. 'The bull's still running with them so we'll try her again next time you come.'

I started to tip the bucket of water down my calving gown, rinsing off the dark-staining cow muck which inevitably gets everywhere, especially while the cows are at summer grazing.

'I'll tell you a funny thing,' he continued. 'Do you remember that cow's foot you looked at in the summer? We had them all in the yard this morning to get these few out, and do you know, I couldn't recognise her for a bit – had me really foxed. Then it suddenly dawned on me which one she was; she's an absolute picture now and the foot looks completely normal. I had a bit of a shock when the bill came but she certainly looks worth it now. Quite remarkable.'

When I got back to the surgery later in the day, I asked Pauline to look up the record on that cow, wanting, I suppose, to enjoy a little longer the glow of satisfaction when an animal does well. 'Ah – here she is,' said Pauline, her finger on a line in the day book, 'July 7th – Hargreaves Boothroyd – miracle job needed on cow's foot.'

She had written down the phone message verbatim. I rubbed my chin for a moment. Now that's a strange way to request a visit, I mused.

On Reflection

Most of us are able to picture, in our mind's eye, a scene containing a ship within the calm waters of a lake or estuary. As it moves slowly through the water, it leaves behind a wake, at first churned water behind the propeller, and later, small eddies and whirlpools in an otherwise strangely polished surface, stretching out behind the ship for hundreds of yards.

Most of us also know the opening words of the 23rd psalm, 'The Lord is my shepherd . . . ' but later, it ends with the words, 'Surely, goodness and mercy shall follow me all the days of my life, and I will dwell in the house of the Lord for ever.' (Authorised Version) Now I know that most modern translations of the Bible say 'goodness and love,' instead of 'goodness and mercy,' but the older version seems more appropriate to animals.

Jesus tells us to be 'salt and light', i.e. to make a difference to the world in which we live, whether that's the world of work, the micro-world of our home and family, or the world at large. I like to harbour the secret thought that Christians should be like ships, quietly leaving some mark of the Kingdom of God in their wake, discernable to those with eyes to see it.

If we have the great privilege to be in one of the healing professions, then our path through life should automatically leave relief of suffering in its wake, but outside our professional lives, we all have the same opportunity to influence the lives of others, in our conversation and in simple acts of helpfulness or kindness. If we do this, not in a deliberate, overt manner, but quite naturally, as a way of life, then we mustn't be too surprised if we see one of God's little miracles now and again.

'Surely, goodness and mercy shall follow me all the days of my life, . . .'

CHAPTER NINE

We All Like Sheep

IT WAS A LARGER-THAN-LIFE Malcolm who appeared in the doorway of our little office, face flushed with the heat of a man who'd been overdoing things. Without any regard for the ambience of the room, he strode in, landed a box of used syringes on the desk and dropped himself into the nearest chair.

'Am I glad it's your turn on duty tonight,' he said, glancing at Roger with eyes like a raptor's. 'I've just about had enough of this week.'

Pauline, Roger and I had been enjoying a lull at the end of the day, engaged in a pleasant exchange of light conversation. I say 'had been' because clearly, Malcolm wasn't going to lose a moment in unburdening the tribulations of his week.

'On Tuesday night, I had a cow stuck in a cubicle at Jim Hardie's. There was only him and that skinny lad of his. If he turned sideways on he nearly vanished! Not much help as Jim and I heaved and strained to slide the cow out. 'Course, it was fairly toxic with mastitis so I had to give it a drip. It was so gloomy I could hardly find the vein and the whole business took far too long. That meant I had a late tea and I was just going to bed when Jenny Hackforth rang to say her horse was choked. Turned out it had got some dry sugar beet with its evening feed and when I got there, it was still coughing and retching, trying to clear itself. An hour and a half that took before I finally got it cleared.'

'Did you give it some Spasmocaine?' Roger interjected. 'I always find an intravenous dose of that clears them pretty quickly.'

'*'Course* I gave it some,' exclaimed Malcolm vehemently, leaning well forward in his chair now, '*and* some atropine *and* some sedative! Complete waste of time. It was a stomach tube and flushing job and I thought it would never clear.'

Roger looked suitably chastened, and Pauline and I exchanged the most discreet of knowing glances.

'On Wednesday,' he went on with his catalogue, 'some fathead in a van ran into the back of me at Boothroyd junction and bent the back door so I haven't been able to get into the boot ever since. A real pain reaching over the back seat all the time.'

Pauline got up at this point and went to the end of the bench to put the kettle on. 'Tea or coffee, Malcolm?' she asked.

'Strong coffee with two sugars,' came the instant reply. 'Thanks,' as an afterthought. 'Then this afternoon,' he went on, 'at David Wheeler's, instead of four horses for registration, he produced seven. Jolly lucky I had enough forms with me, and standing in his yard drawing all those socks and whorls was absolutely perishing.'

Pauline handed over the freshly brewed coffee. 'This'll put you right,' she said, and Malcolm clasped the mug in both hands, extracting comfort from the warmth and aroma.

'If it's any consolation, Malcolm,' I said slowly, taking advantage of the pause, 'I'd spent nearly two hours blood testing McWirter's cows and preg. testing his heifers when he presented me with this bullock which kept getting bloat. He'd been letting it down with a stomach tube for nearly a week so I had no option but to do a rumen fistula op. My hands were all stained from holding tails and all he could manage was one washing-up bowl of water for the whole job! Not the most sterile operation I've ever done!'

I could tell by the way Malcolm was looking through me, that he didn't find it much consolation. 'Still,' I added, turning to Roger, 'at least he won't be phoning you tonight, "We 'ave this bullock...",' I mimicked.

Malcolm shifted his position in the chair and swallowed some more coffee. Roger looked distinctly uncomfortable. 'I hate to remind you,' he began, shifting his gaze onto the floor, 'but can you remember asking if I'd mind swapping nights?'

'Oh no,' Malcolm interjected, 'Rachel's birthday on Tuesday so I'm going out for a meal.'

'So you asked if you could be "on" tonight instead of me,' Roger continued, but not daring to let a smile cross his face. Malcolm slumped back in his chair and Pauline collected her things and put her coat on, ready for home.

'Well,' she said, with a shrug of her shoulders and a smile, 'I'll be off now – see you all in the...' The telephone cut her short, and she stopped in the doorway.

'You get off home, Pauline, you're late enough as it is,' I said. 'I'll answer it.'

Malcolm put his empty mug on the bench, and an anxious look spread across his tired features. I picked up the phone. 'Colston Veterinary Centre,' I answered routinely. It was the stableyard at Deansworth Lodge.

'When do you think it happened, Mrs Blake?... About dinner time...'

Malcolm stared sightlessly at the floor with an air of resignation.

'How deep is the cut?' I asked... 'Well, if you think you can see bone exposed, yes, of course we'll come this evening. Whose horse is it, by the way?' I took down the owner's details and then reassured Mrs Blake that we'd be there within the hour and asked her to make sure that the yard light was left on.

'Sorry, Malcolm,' I said, replacing the receiver, 'I really couldn't let that one wait until the morning. Mrs Blake at Deansworth stables – horse with a gashed shoulder. They didn't know about it until they brought it in from the field just now.'

'OK, OK, fair enough,' said Malcolm, struggling to his feet, 'I'll be on my way. All part of the cheerful service,' he added, but without much evidence of cheer!

'Tell you what,' said Roger, launching himself out of the chair, 'I'll go and see the horse. You go home, have a shower and something to eat, and then you'll be OK if anything else comes in.

'No, honestly,' said Malcolm, 'I was being a bit silly – I'm better after that coffee.'

'No matter,' said Roger, reaching for his car keys, 'you look all in. I'll soon put a stitch or two in the horse so off you go, while I'm feeling generous.' With that, he was through the door and away into the twilight.

We'll leave the vets' office now, their day's work and all the characters they meet. We'll leave the animals they have been discussing, and all the farmyards, stables and fields where many others have been receiving their professional attention for one reason or another.

We'll go instead to a market town in the East Riding of Yorkshire and look again at the work of George Carter, the preacher and evangelist we met at the beginning of the book. His work took him to many different churches over a wide area of the country and quite often, he never found out the results of his labours. Sometimes, however, news reached him of lives which had been changed in many different ways, partly at least because of his inspiring teaching. We'll join him in the sitting room of Sally Edmondson which she has made available for a meeting for a group of young people. Some of them come from Christian homes, and some are there just out of curiosity. George is leading the meeting, talking to them in his usual compelling manner, this time about the passage in Mark's gospel where Jesus and the disciples cross Lake Galilee in a boat to try and find some peace and quiet on the other side. As it turned out, however, the crowds had got there first!

'When Jesus landed, and saw a large crowd,' he read, 'he had compassion on them, because they were like sheep without a shepherd. So he began teaching them many things.'

'Now,' said George, putting his Bible on the floor beside him, and sitting well forward in his armchair, 'who can remember their first week at primary school?' A giggle went round the group of teenagers and broad smiles were exchanged as they recollected their experiences of ten or eleven years previously. 'It all seems a long time ago, doesn't it?' George went on, 'but can you cast your minds back and remember when your Mum or Dad left you at the playground gate and said, "'bye Darren," or "'bye Samantha"?'

There was an outburst of laughter as, by chance, a boy called Darren was in the group. He blushed as somebody teased him about once losing his coat in the school cloakroom. George spared the poor lad's embarrassment by hastily pursuing his theme.

'Do you remember how older children befriended you and, sooner or later, a teacher called you into school, showed you the cloakroom,' – more giggles – 'and eventually gathered you into the classroom? It was quite an unnerving experience at the time, wasn't it?' There were just enough nods of agreement to allow him to proceed.

'Right,' he said, changing the direction of the conversation, 'have you ever been going along in the car in springtime, and seen a couple of naughty lambs that got out into the road and couldn't find their way back?'

'That happened to me an' Carl when we were out on our bikes,' said a youth called Edward, all eyes turning towards him. 'We found a gate we could open and managed to get them back in,' he concluded with a satisfied smile.

'Ah, but was it the right field?' asked George mischievously.

The group had a good laugh while Edward's smile vanished into his cupped hands, emerging broader than ever after a couple of seconds.

'Let's try again,' continued the evangelist. 'Have you ever been going along in the car and met a whole flock of sheep that's strayed into the road?'

Nobody could quite recall such an incident so, to smother the silence, George painted a word picture of the scene for them. Disorientated sheep milling nervously around, one or two bolt for an imagined gap in the fence, and a few follow till they see the leading individuals bounce back into the road. The milling becomes more agitated as they realise that sheep at the other side of the flock are now heading off up the road in the opposite direction. With much bleating, they all start to follow, funnelling into a running river of woolly-backs, but panic (here, George enlivened the word picture with some exaggerated body language, his arms flailing in mock confusion) panic, a car is coming up the other way and the leading sheep are turning round and running back along the verges.

The young people's vivid imaginations took them right to the scene and there were a few derogatory remarks about mutton-heads. George picked up his Bible, relaxed back into his chair and said, 'OK, who would like to volunteer to read a verse of scripture?'

At first, nobody would, but in the light-hearted atmosphere

that had been generated, a couple of girls soon pointed out that one of the boys called Nathan was a good reader.

'Well done, Nathan,' said George with a grin, 'you've just been volunteered to read a bit of the Old Testament,' and handing over the Bible, he pointed out a verse in Isaiah. The hapless Nathan hesitated a moment, scanned the lines and, taking a deep breath, began to read in sonorous tones,

'We all like sheep,' he began, at which the meeting dissolved in mirth, partly at the unexpected funny, and partly to further embarrass poor Nathan, who, still serious, hadn't yet caught up with the joke. George stilled the laughter by asking with a broad smile, 'Doesn't it say, "We all, comma, like sheep, comma, have gone astray," Nathan?' The young people loved the sudden alteration of the meaning and instantly let the giggles subside in order to let Nathan have another go.

'We all,' he paused, 'like sheep,' another pause, 'have gone astray; each of us has turned to his own way.'

'Thank you, Nathan,' said George, reaching out to retrieve his Bible. A more respectable hush filled the room now and the teenagers wondered what was coming next. 'You see,' he went on, more seriously now, 'the Bible says that left to our own devices, we're a bit like those sheep. We're very apt to stray onto highways and byeways which we'd be better off avoiding. Some roads we take in life get us into trouble. Some roads just get us nowhere and waste a lot of our time. The trouble is,' he went on, 'we're not always very good at recognising which way is the one we ought to be taking.'

He paused to allow the youngsters time to reflect on these ideas, and was gratified to see that nobody looked like arguing. Then, in brighter style he announced, 'So, what we need is someone like a shepherd who takes it upon himself to guide and, well, shepherd the sheep along the right pathways. Now,' he said, looking round the room, 'who was it who said Nathan was a good reader?'

'Elaine,' someone said.

'Ah, good,' said George. 'You'll be Elaine, I take it,' he said, and smiling sweetly at his next volunteer went on, 'I wonder if you'd be so kind as to read our next quotation?' and he passed his Bible across, now marked at a passage in the New Testament.

Abashed as she was, Elaine was obliged to accept the book, clearly unaccustomed to looking at those long columns of print, peppered as they were with the numbers of chapter and verse. With her finger firmly on the place, she drew breath and began to read.

'I am the good shepherd,' she began. 'The good shepherd lays down his life for the sheep . . .' She stumbled over a line, but there was no teasing now as everyone wanted to listen, and she soon reached the end of the passage. 'I know my sheep and my sheep know me – just as the Father knows me and I know the Father – and,' she stumbled again, 'and I lay down my life for the sheep.'

Out of the moment's silence which followed, George spoke quietly.

'Does anyone know who the good shepherd might be?'

'Jesus?' someone offered, tentatively.

'Quite right,' answered George, 'Jesus Christ himself. Can you think,' he asked, engaging their imaginations once more, 'can you think of when a shepherd might endanger his life for the sake of the flock?' It didn't take long for somebody to remember the flooding of a few months ago when acres of farmland had disappeared under water.

'One farmer had to be rescued by helicopter after he got stuck trying to move his sheep onto higher land,' said the youth earnestly.

WE ALL LIKE SHEEP

'You sometimes hear about blizzards, 'specially in Scotland,' said another, 'and farmers have to go out and see to the sheep – that could be dangerous if it was at night.'

'That's the sort of thing,' answered George, 'somebody doing their job, even in the face of danger to themselves, to try to save others, whether it's sheep or,' he hesitated, 'people.' Pausing a moment, he reached over for Elaine to return his Bible.

'Jesus says here,' he read, '"I lay down my life for the flock."' What did he mean by "lay down my life," do you think?' He looked round for an answer and after a few seconds, one of the girls said very shyly, 'Was it about him being crucified?'

George nodded, 'It's a horrible word, isn't it,' he said, 'but yes, you're quite right, Jesus knew he would soon be put to a cruel death at the hands of Roman soldiers. That's the bad news,' he smiled, 'but the good news,' his smile broadened, 'is that three days later, God brought him back to life, a life which we, as believers, can share!'

Some of the group seemed to accept this easily, while others began to look a little incredulous.

'Listen to what St. Paul wrote,' George said excitedly, hastily flicking over some pages. '"The life I live in the body,"' he read, '"I live by faith in the Son of God who loved me and gave his life for me." Gave *his* life for me,' he repeated. 'That's a humbling thought isn't it? Or, looking at it another way, "gave his life – for *me*"!' At that moment, there was a knock on the door and Sally, the willing hostess, appeared with a trolley full of goodies.

'Sorry to interrupt,' she said, hesitantly, 'but I've got a few refreshments ready if you'd like some.'

Smiles of surprise and delight answered the question more eloquently than George's assertion that her timing couldn't have been better, and with this encouragement, she negotiated her way through to the centre of the room and proudly presented her assortment of drinks, cakes and biscuits.

'I hope there'll be enough,' she said. 'Feeding teenagers is like feeding the five thousand!'

'I'm sure there'll be plenty to go round,' said George, with evident anticipation, 'and while we're enjoying them,' he continued, facing the group once again, 'it'll be a good opportunity to ask any questions you may have, and I'll do my best to answer them for you. But before we all tuck in, we must thank Sally for going to all this trouble for us – it really is a mouth-watering spread – and just to bring the formal part of the afternoon to a close, can we just join together in a short prayer.'

Everyone bowed their heads to give an impression of reverence.

'Almighty God,' he said boldly, 'thank you for the good fellowship we've enjoyed here this afternoon, and for what we've learned about sheep and shepherds. Thank you that you teach us about godliness in simple pictures from everyday life. I pray that these pictures may find a place in our hearts and that as we seek you, we may indeed receive that new life which you give through your son, our Saviour, Jesus Christ. Amen.'

'Amen,' was the muttered reply, and within a moment or two, the chattering was unleashed and Sally's trolley was being rapidly unloaded.

'Mr Carter?' asked a serious voice.

'Yes,' said George, whipping round to face the boy who had squatted down beside him.

'Well . . .' he went on earnestly, 'do animals go to heaven . . . ?'